Doll Making
as a
Transformative Process

Pamela Hastings

© 2003 and 2015

www.pamelahastings.com

Illustrations by Pamela Hastings

Photographs by Allen Bryan, Pamela Hastings, and the Contributors

Other Pamela Hastings publications include:

Hot Flash! A Celebration

Paper Dolls Inspiration Art

Altered Books

Fabric Journals

3-D Doll Construction

Designing a Doll and Making Faces Inspiration Book

Dedication

This book is for Mom, who did the best she could to encourage and nurture my creativity, and for providing me with transformative work to do.

For Elinor Peace Bailey and Lenore Davis, who expanded everyone's understanding of what doll makking could be.

And for all the people in this book and around the world who share their stories.

This book is for you and with you; the journey never ends and we are on it together.

Table of Contents

Patterns

Introduction

The study of doll making as a transformative process, using art as a tool to facilitate and record life change, is ever-evolving. Because the technology of electronic books now allows for full color and the ability to send this book anywhere without prohibitive postage costs, I created a second edition, which combines the original book, the material from my online classes, additional patterns and materials from more contributors and from ideas cultural themes that have evolved in over a decade since the original book in 2003.

The stories and suggestions in this book are based on my and other's personal experiences. There are no guarantees offered about any specific outcomes. Physical or mental difficulties respond to a wide range of professional and other treatments. Please consult a trusted professional in combination with any of the techniques described in this book.

Women offer each other stories as a way of bonding, whereas men seem to share lists of accomplishments. The resurgence of journaling, decorative and home-centered arts, and even narrative medicine is a response to big business, big agriculture, greedy haphazard genetic engineering, big corporation-directed government, big religious mindless aggression toward women and children, and the imminent threats to all life on earth, even more so now than a decade ago. I believe we are trying to heal the planet and ourselves in more gentle, low tech, and introspective ways, including sharing in groups as an age-old method of dispensing knowledge and support. I believe I am doing what older women are supposed to do—making my own experience available in order to leave the world a better place for those who come after.

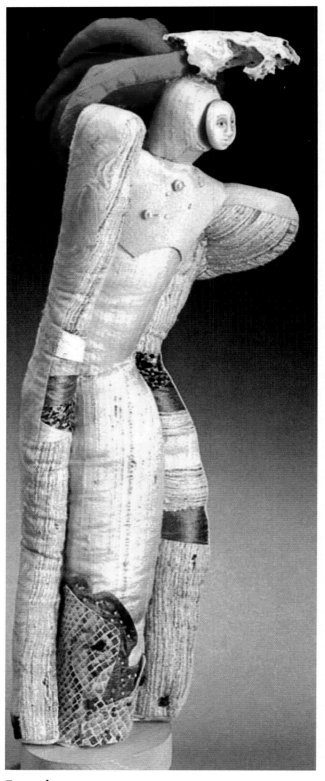

Emerging
1998 14" UltraSuede, animal skull, beads, and ivory face

I started a conscious journey of self-discovery at age twenty when I started keeping a journal with words and drawing. As a child, I remember looking at light on water and wondering how to paint it. I made illustrated stories in black and white marbleized-cover essay books. I have always been an artist of words and images. Through my participation in Making Creative Cloth Dolls with Lark Press, I discovered how cumbersome the process of working with a large company can be, and how huge a number of books must be sold to consider the project a success, diluting its thrust. By publishing my own books, I can tell the stories in my own way, and now with e-Books, I can add to and change each edition. By using my own dolls and life as the thread of the story, I hope to set a Permission Example for you to tell your own story freely. Because mostly women have been interested in this process, I will address you as females and students, though I know that you may go on as therapists to use these techniques with your clients. Please feel free to email me, *pamela@pamelahastings.com* if there are points you wish to discuss as a student, creator, or therapist.

A more open discussion of our own challenging times leads to more interpersonal support and de-mystification, fewer lonely and isolated abused women, and fewer overwhelmed parents,. more open discussion of the environment, gender identification and bullying. Everything that we experience teaches and modifies us. We have the power to choose how we use this experience, in positive or negative ways, building a stronger or weaker self with which to meet future life challenges.

Making art—anything that we design with creative intention, makes more energy than the sum of its parts. Doing this work in groups creates even more energy. Imagine groups all over the world creating Art and influencing the future, saving the planet for our children and grandchildren. Draw, wrap, imagine, sew your way out of old ruts until all the dark secrets are dissipated and lose their power to do harm.

Inherited Nightmare (In Progress)
I built the form in muslin then painted it with watered-down acrylic paints.

I am especially grateful to Barb Kobe for sharing decades of research and teaching on this topic. We will each publish books in early summer of 2015—a consolidation of each life's work. I bristle at the numbers of authors who try to convince potential customers/readers that something is wrong with you and only they can fix it. We are partners in this quest for resolution and ease in our lives, increased understanding of our history and clearer insight in planning our futures.

The material has been used by individuals and in Art Therapy programs around the world and now the advance in technology that allows for e-books has made it possible to include information from additional contributors, as well as material that was not as much in the public eye at the beginning of the Twenty-First Century as it is now, such as sexual and national identity. Aging didn't concern me as much as it does now. The Slow Food Movement started in Italy in 1986 as a protest against construction of *McDonalds*. Now there is Slow Knitting, a resurgence of Farmers' Markets, meditation, and perhaps a rising appreciation for deep work that is touched by human hands, along with the meditative benefits of beading and stitching.

I started this Transformative way of working by noticing how much I used art an doll making in my own personal journey and how common and how effective it can be. Join me and the other artists represented here, to expand your own repertoire of tools for life change.

We each create our own personal experience and interpretation of reality, our own unique universe.

You'll find resources and links on the last pages.
pamela@pamelahastings.com
Students and teachers please contact me.

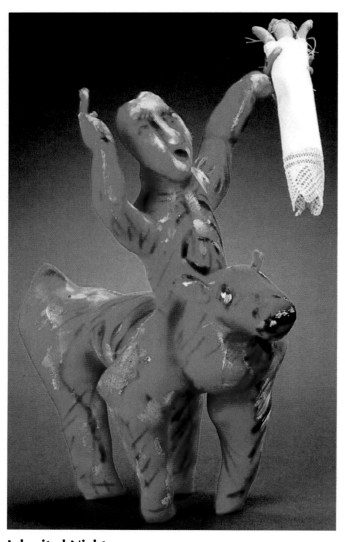

Inherited Nightmare

2003 16″ Muslin with acrylic paint. The small figure's dress is the edge of a family pillow case

Doll making, in the larger sense of cloth dolls and journals, paper dolls, painting, writing, drawing, and collage saved my life. Guess that got your attention. I was a typical abused wife, living in a remote area, an old schoolhouse in the Northeast Kingdom of Vermont, with an insecure and violent husband. I was raised in the Fifties to believe that the husband is always right, but subversively, I started using art making, including a series on the ritual suicide of writer *Yukio Mishima*, to express the anger and frustration I was not yet ready to express directly in my relationship.

I invite you to participate in this process of Transformation, believing that what we need will show up when we need it, even if it's not exactly what we think we want. Each person is born with a unique capacity for creativity. If you don't give voice to yours, it will wither. Un-expressed strong emotions and suppressed memories can fester, causing physical problems.

The book is arranged in chapters, working from individual transformation, to transforming the world. There are patterns and suggestions for activities throughout. The exercises will come together in different ways for different readers at different stages in your lives. When we create our experience of reality in a concrete form, through a doll or other symbolic work the finished product is not necessarily a work of art, but a functional tool to help us see our own lives and goals more clearly.

The doll you create is NOT YOU. It is a vehicle for making the invisible visible and therefore easier to change. At times scary, ugly, or unpleasant images and words may come pouring from your hands. This is a good thing, and not a sign that you should be immediately institutionalized. We all contain a whole Pandora's Box of Gremlins, but in the safe environment of doll making we can take the little suckers out to play.

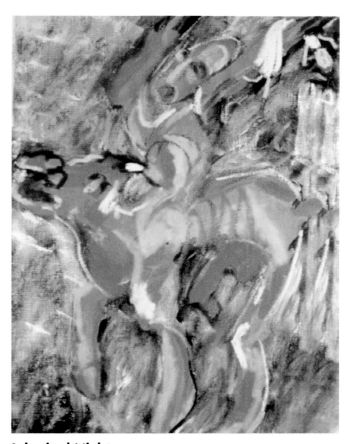

Inherited Nightmare
Preliminary mixed-media drawing. A quick and messy-mixed drawing can be a way to access emotions, then translate them to a more finished work.

After we create them, we have the power to accept and acknowledge them and go on about our lives with greater freedom. We can decide if we want to continue to haul this baggage around with us for the rest of our lives, or salute the stuff and put it to rest, transforming anger into energy for change, the sadness into a full range of feeling, the despair into hope for small possibilities.

Do Transformative Doll Making without waiting to be in the mood. It will get easier. The more you do, the more ideas you will find coming to the surface and the easier it will be to access the buried feelings. Simple forms can express strong emotions more effectively than realism. Start with what you have physically and emotionally. Limitations in structure and skill breed creativity in approach and execution.

Where does your Inner Critic/Voice of Judgement come from—is it your mother, an old teacher, general insecurity about the validity of your own feelings? How will you silence your Critic—at least for the time it takes to create—half an hour? What does your pain look like? Can you decorate it, deck it out, make it smaller, or create a larger, comforting figure to embrace you and sooth your pain? Sit quietly for a few moments and visualize freeing yourself from the constricting corset of your ego and overwhelming self-awareness.

In *Melzack and Wall's gate-control theory* of pain management, there is only so much space for information to enter our neural pathways at one time. TENS electronic pain management units work by producing a neutral electric buzz that makes it harder for the pain messages to get through the nerves. Occupational Therapists and Art Therapists use a focus on pleasurable and absorbing activities to block out the emotional and physical messages of pain. Becoming totally engrossed in doll making works to block self-defeating messages from the psyche and can also help to distract the participant from physical hurt. The power of extremely simple forms is evident in *Andrea Cooley's* poem (p.71), as are the multiple layers of meaning possible in combinations of simple forms. For beginning doll makers, concentrating on simple forms allows the emotional message to take supremacy.

Throughout the book, I'll give you suggestions for using the power of doll making—a very powerful medium—in your own transformative process.

Child is Father to the Man
2003 16″ Soft sculpture with paper and china faces in an antique drawer

Cultures throughout history have used the doll form for Transformative purposes, as icons that mediate between this world and the spirit world, sending positive—or negative—thoughts for one's self or another. For luck in the hunt, to grow good crops, to banish disease, or bring harm to an enemy.

The aim in this process is not to make Great Art, although we see Art Dolls everywhere now that the internet brings Everything in the World to our desk tops. For those who have the will or the background, design principles can certainly be applied, but I prefer not to have that foremost in your mind when using doll making for Transformative purposes. The conscious effort of making a "beautiful" or "artistic" piece can interfere horribly with allowing your Subconscious to play with materials and perform unexpected feats for your amazement and amusement. "The work of creativity is not a matter of making the material come, but of unblocking the obstacles to is natural flow," says *Stephen Nachmanovitch* in *Free Play*.

Try to approach your materials with no preconceived notion about what will come out. Let the dance between your eyes, hands, colors, fabrics, and shapes take you where it will. Above all, silence your Inner Critic, and watch to see what happens. Whatever meditation practice is comfortable to you can help to clear you Monkey Mind before you begin. Limit your choices of materials to avoid distraction. I find that being alone in the house helps when I'm doing this work.

To Begin: gather 4-6 materials that speak to you, an object, a phrase. I used to use TV for background noise, sometimes a boring book on tape or classical music—an aural way of increasing focus—you'll know what works best for you. Another way to encourage ideas to rise is to keep a sketch pad handy while doing a repetitive task such as folding clothes, shelling peas, weeding. I let my mind wander with in gardening, walking, or driving—pull over first, please).

It can be helpful to have rituals for beginning and ending a Tranformative session. The rituals put your subconscious in a receptive frame. The ceremony can be as simple as a moment of quiet breathing and relaxation or putting the piece-in-process in a special place where you can see it during your daily movement around the house.

Mother What Did You Want?
2003 12″ Soft sculpture with paper and ceramic faces. Note the orange arm/connection between the figures.

Shawn McNiff PhD, teacher and writer about Expressive Therapy, likes to use movement as a warm-up for the whole body. You may find yourself making different types of marks and shapes if your whole body is energized than if your are stiff and stodgy from the end of the work day. Transformation and Creativity are linked in my thinking, plucking up ideas from *Jung's Collective Unconscious* and putting them into concrete form. Is all creativity Transformative? Not necessarily. It can depend on intention. Sometimes I'm just playing with shape, color, texture, and image. Sometimes it's only later that I can read the subconscious content.

As I work, I allow myself to get tired and rest, perhaps by doing some contemplative decorative beading or hanging the laundry. I run away, walk, rest, and bring myself back to the practice. Like any sport or skill, this gets easier with practice. Start first with a very simple form.

DREAM JOURNAL: Keep a book and pen by your bed to use to write your dreams, then whatever thoughts may spool off from thinking about your dreams, since dreams represent a letting go of every day reality. I write so much that I keep a journal on computer plus books for design.

I must admit that often my dreams are rather boring re-creations of whatever happened the day before, but the format of dreams is a useful way to get into the unconscious creative process. As in dreams, there is no logical progression involved. You may see new ideas emerging, new ways of interpreting an event that seemed nonsensical at first glance, or images that you can now see in new ways. Tune out the other people in the room and the Ego Self who usually keeps a tight rein on your awareness. Let the work guide you where it wants to go.

Do multiple pieces on the same theme to reveal new levels of meaning and understanding, like peeling an onion. People talk about the same life experiences for years in therapy, so don't worry about time. The doll making process will be much more fun and also give you a tangible end product. Or you may use Transformative Doll Making in conjunction with talk therapy, as Art Therapist, *Lani Gerity (p.124)* has done. Unravel your negative self-talk and re-knit positive stories and images for yourself.

Doll Based on Primitive Forms
2003 8″ The face is a smashed and rusty found metal piece. No need to worry about realistic features.

There are many stories of breakthroughs in therapy, in spiritual practice, in using painting as therapy. I have had my own "clicking into place" moments, often with words as a component or culmination of a series of dolls or images. Anything visual: dolls, written words, fabric or paper journals, especially when you let the finished project sit where you see it for a while, can lead to insights. Automatic writing or letting words flow freely while contemplating your finished piece may lead to break throughs. This could be part of a life-long process of investigation and discovery, a life-time supply of all the material you need for your art career. That is the case for me.

Like the Buddhists, I see the Entire Universe in my own small part of it. Don't expect Grand Break Throughs, followed by Happily Ever After. Life is a long corridor, with doors opening at intervals, spiral staircases going up and down.

The process does not have to be agonizing and gut wrenching, although it may feel that way at times. As we play with our wonderful colors and textures, found objects, and other materials, doll making can be an enjoyable way to observe our sometimes hidden selves, to laugh at past fears, to celebrate our current selves, and our selves-to-be. With ceremony and support in modern versions of sewing circles, we share experiences, validation, and knowledge, and emerge as stronger and happier people with more energy to apply to our dreams, enjoying our lives in every moment.

Everything in the World

1996 20" A figure made for a Healing Art Show. Painted muslin, decorated with beads and ultra suede leaves, the words "Everything in the World written on the body, me thinking about all my friends with AIDS and what they would miss. Fortunately their future is less bleak now.

Again, the stories and suggestions in this book are based on each teller's personal experiences. There are no guarantees offered about any specific outcomes. Physical or mental difficulties respond to a wide range of professional and other treatments.

Please consult a trusted professional in combination with any of the the techniques mentioned in this book. There is no shame in asking for help.

I have been an artist, drawing and making up stories in black and white composition books since I was five and dictated stories to my mother. In looking back on my own history in 2003, I saw how much I'd used the doll construction, drawing, and painting as away to understand and get in touch with my own emotions, to look at situations in my own life, such as serial abusive relationships. I saw how much art work was helping me to change my life and attitudes and it seemed really important to share all this, in case I could help other women.

We moved a lot when I was a child, as my father was stationed at different VA Hospitals. I made dolls and doll clothes to have something to do to compensate for my social ineptitude and to have a project while Dad was driving us around to find the perfect place from which to take photos of trains. I was drawn to Dad's cool books on the artwork of psychotic patients. My mother wanted me to learn a profession so I would not be dependent on a man to support me, so I pursued the practical course of Occupational Therapy, which did use arts and crafts in the Sixties. I studied lots of psychology. Even though I soon didn't use the arts at work, I kept quitting health care to make a living doing craft shows until I had to go back to work to give myself hope of eventual retirement.

I made *Edith Flack Ackley* inspired costume dolls in high school, costumed the community theater, found Soft Sculpture in the Seventies, with Lenore Davis' story pieces. Since I was already making paintings with acrylics on canvas, it was a short step to paint on muslin for soft sculpture. Your transformative work will reflect the tools you have developed to create your art work. I have included projects on paper, quick projects, and ones that require no sewing to meet different skill levels. In the Transformative Process, the process is more important than the product.

It Is In Me, But Not Of Me

1997 24″ Made for a Healing Art Exhibit. Pieced fabric, lace, beads, antique rattle that can be rotated to show a pink face. Expresses the idea that ill health is not the whole person. This is also part of a series in which I work on boundary setting with my mother, an ongoing process.

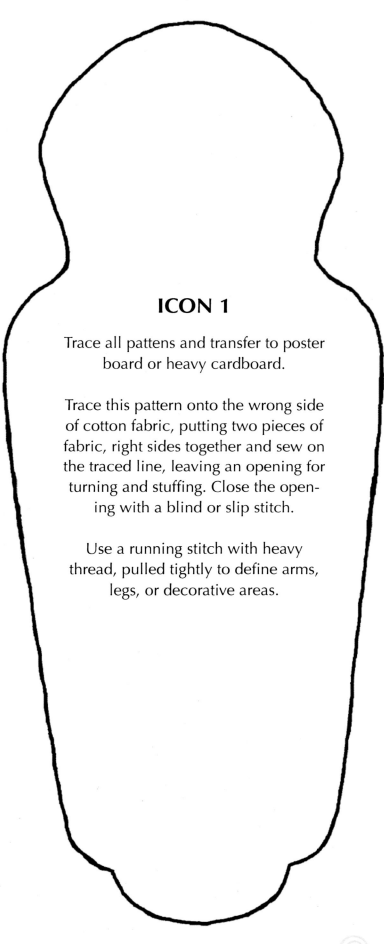

ICON 1

Trace all pattens and transfer to poster board or heavy cardboard.

Trace this pattern onto the wrong side of cotton fabric, putting two pieces of fabric, right sides together and sew on the traced line, leaving an opening for turning and stuffing. Close the opening with a blind or slip stitch.

Use a running stitch with heavy thread, pulled tightly to define arms, legs, or decorative areas.

Vision Icon

2008 9″ To focus my hope for slowed deterioration of my retinas. Velvet (backed with iron-on interfacing for stability), embroidered intention, eyes drawn on cotton fabric, trim, beads, a button and eye-shaped talismans. A small ring on the back for hanging. So far my vision is decreasing slowly.

Transformative History

There's an age-old history of using dolls and icons for Transformative purposes—anthropomorphic spirits that mediate between this world and the other-worldly. Ancient representations of Goddesses instill cultural values by instruction and ritual in early Greece, Australia, Africa, and the South Pacific. Mexican *Milagros*, silver charms, represent prayers for the health of specific body parts, a practice that continues into the modern-day custom of leaving crutches and artificial limbs in Catholic shrines, as I've seen in the Cathedral in Montreal.

In the *Vodou* religion, in both Africa and the Caribbean, all living things, all objects in nature, are intertwined so tightly that what one does to an image or a doll also happens, for good or ill, to who or what that doll represents. Suggestion and belief have proven to be very powerful forces and not just for supposedly primitive people. After working in Health Care for 25 years, I KNOW that we don't know all there is to know about how healing and transformation work. The ritual and ceremony of modern health care, including doctors wearing white coats, medicine tasting bad, and costing a lot, the Focus on a desired outcome can turn that energy into something powerful. People make themselves sick with worry, as well as using mental energy for healing.

Masks use art as the mediator between Humanity and our terrors. Some of our fears today may be different, but no less real to us. The march of time makes us feel less and less in control of our futures, our work lives, our environment, our children's futures, our security in the continuity of our relationships, world events striking closer to home, and climate changing.

In more modern days dolls like Barbie and her ilk, GI Joe and Power Rangers are/were used in mass marketing to imprint cultural roles like mother, warrior, sexual stereotype, and instill in children the desire for greater consumption. However, dolls can also be a way to examine these stereotypes and act out sexual roles to learn more about our assumptions. An altered version of the norm can lead to an examination of what we accept as normal. How is your doll version of yourself different from the average? Now, in more enlightened cultures sexual identity can exist on a continuum, instead of just pink and blue. Are there parts of your own character at odds with your cultural standards? Can you celebrate your own diversity in a doll version of your Super Heroine self?

Double-headed

6.5″ Wooden figure purchased at a flea market, doubtless intended as an object of power, possibly African or Caribbean. Simple and strong shapes and features.

Many use fairy tales as archetypal stories. To which fairy tales do you respond especially strongly? *Clarissa Pinkola Estes* is an especially well-known Jungian analyist who connects the folk tales of many cultures with helping her clients work through traumas. Our cultural stories are lessons about life principles and which types of behavior are rewarded. Those of us who grew up in the Fifties were very strongly pressured to conform, and there are still those in some religions and political arenas who seem to want to keep women barefoot and pregnant.

When you act out the Good Girl/Bad Girl myths in a safe setting with doll making, isn't the truth somewhere in the middle? Dolls, uncensored and uninhibited, like childhood play and masquerade, give us a safe place to try on, modify, or discard forbidden roles that only exert a more powerful pull when they are suppressed. Doll play is safe. "Almost all religions include what some anthropologists call 'transformative practices,' that is, acts which when performed properly by humans, mobilize "supernatural' forces in order to affect human life." write Sidney Mintz & Michel-Rolph Trouillot in T*he Sacred Arts of Haitian Vodou.*

A technique that we inherited from ancient times and still find helpful in the Transformative process is repetitive story telling (rehashing past images until they no longer have the power to frighten us or to drive our lives in the form of a dark, un-examined undertone). Stories told over and over with slight improvements can be a talisman to keep the demons at bay, and because image making of dolls and icons exists at an even earlier and more primal level of communication than words, they can still function as exorcism, defined here as creating a simple physical representation of the traumatic event, fear, or person. We can truly see how much stronger we are now than that piece of past. We can stage a symbolic burning or burial. Or we can create serial figures, gradually transforming the object of fear into a way of perceiving the positive aspects of our own strength in surviving past or inherited experiences, providing an alternative story and nurturing for ourselves. At 68, I am becoming my own Good Mother.

Edith Flack Ackley
1963 10″ She taught women in the Fifties to make costume dolls for income. These are some of mine from when I was in high school. I used doll making instead of hanging out with friends, since I was always the New Kid.

My first Puppet Princes
1952 12″ My first doll. I always wanted to live in a girly fantasy world. Writing stories, creating dolls and puppets allowed me to indulge that desire, although I also wanted to be the sheriff and capture Bad Guys.

Telling stories, making dolls or drawings or fabric journal pages in groups is powerful, like our ancestors sitting around a campfire, we share our personal histories, learn we are not alone ,and are safe in experimenting with different roles and outcomes to our pasts.

In each person's developmental history, the concept of PLAY and Permission to Play, non-serious self-discovery, playing with others, sharing insights and toys is a mode of creating to which all long to return. The ability to play lies at the heart of all new discovery. Artists and scientists hone their ability to play at will. In the Transformative Doll Groups we create a safe and accepting space in which to play together, banishing the image of the Inner Critic, keeping each other's confidences in a supportive and loving way, emerging at the end of play stronger and more of the person we would like to be, even if we feel we must resume our worldly mask when we leave the safety of the group.

You may elect to use these techniques simply as a way to explore new themes and approaches more intuitively, less self-consciously than in the past. Work at your own individual comfort level and Have Fun, try not to think too much, just Do It. Don't censor. You don't have to show the results to anyone else if you don't want to. When working with clients or in a group, the need for confidentiality should be clearly stated and adhered to.

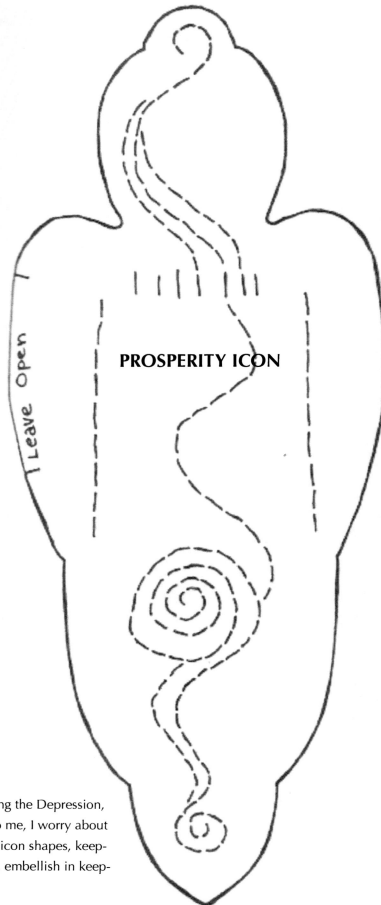

PROSPERITY ICON

Leave Open

Prosperity Icon

Because my mother grew up during the Depression, passing her money scarcity fear to me, I worry about having enough. It's easy to create icon shapes, keeping them simple and symmetrical, embellish in keeping with your focus.

The Goal is to become involved in the process and stay open to what emerges.

You will each come to this process with different goals and needs, and it is fine to go through the projects in whatever depth you wish. At the very least you will discover some fun new patterns and approaches to enlarge your doll making vocabulary. There are projects that can be completed both with and without sewing and at whatever level of art expertise you like.

You can express a lot with a simple shape in fabric. Use whole cloth or create a unique canvas attaching smaller bits of fabric. The two-piece (front and back) type of pattern is simplest to make, but can be very expressive in the way it's embellished and the fabrics you use. When piecing, use short sewing machine stitches and back any fabric that is liable to stretch or fray with iron-on interfacing.

Write an affirmation or intention on a piece of paper or fabric (Sharpies or Fabrico pens are permanent on fabric) and place inside the doll with the stuffing. Meditate on the purpose while completing the piece. A simple running stitch, using several colors of thread in one needle creates a bold graphic line. Use beads, molded faces, no faces, Crayola Model Magic, or paper faces glued to cardboard. A running stitch pulled tightly can delineate arms or legs. Sew a small plastic ring (used for counting knitting stitches) to the back of the head for hanging. Embroider words.

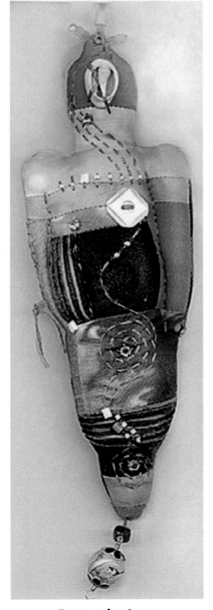

Prosperity Icon

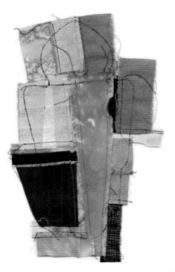

Sew two layers of fabric with right sides together, leaving an opening about 1.5″ long on a straight side, turn and stuff.

Pieced small fabric rectangles, silk is backed with shirt-weight iron-on interfacing, short stitches. Back can be pieced or plain. Trace the pattern on with an Extra Fine Point Sharpie. Sew on the traced line, leaving a 1-2″ opening on a straight side for turning and stuffing.

Arlinka Blair: Tribal Transformation

Arlinka Blair is a doll maker, fiber artist, workshop leader, and artist-in-residence and staff member at Hui Ho'Olana in Molokai, Hawaii. Her work demonstrates a wide-ranging love and appreciation for tribal forms, along with her own unique approach to combining images and ideas. She is as likely to use cloth as paper, a natural shell as a remaindered item from a discount store. She is an excellent example of a soul with a soundly sleeping Inner Critic, and moved to Hawaii when her husband left her. She had traveled with him as he photographed circuses for National Geographic.

"Believe it or not, I have seriously considered shaving my head on more than a few occasions in the past year. I have met really neat and interesting, wonderfully enlightened warm and fuzzy shaved heads. Thinking about the Transformation word I've come to the conclusion that really ALL the dolls are a part of the process of Transformation in one form or another, just different Transformations at different periods in a creative stage.

"On Molokai I have a live-in group-therapy situation daily just with the people on the staff and in the hui community. Working on One's INNER INDEPENDENCE is a very large challenge; and also dealing with long-term changes in one's life, keeping the mind open, adjusting attitude, acceptance, finding new ways to deal with circumstances. Shock has the helpful effect of de-constructing at least momentarily, the neat grid of logic, which forces us to re-examine the ideas in that grid. It is unsettling but comforting in a certain way to know we are all WANDERERS AND STRANGERS in the universe and there is a cosmic structure to which we are meant to relate, if only we could figure it out in this lifetime.

The experience of SIMPLY BEING HERE deepens with each time in Hawaii. Living so closely in Nature with the air and sky, sunshine and light of this island is a wonder."

Orange Paper Doll

Arlinka Blair 10" I took a paper doll class from Arlinka and it totally opened my mind about the unlimited possibilities of paper dolls as art.

Spirit Doll

Arlinka Blair 2002 Her own adaptation of tribal images, feathers, wish bone, decorative stitching.

Spirit Doll

Arlinka Blair 2002 Stuffed fabric shapes, embellished with stitching and paint. Arlinka works with a seamstress to assemble these Spirit Dolls to her specifications.

Paper Doll

Arlinka Blair 2000 14″ With fringe, recycled paper, paint, fabric fringe, stars.

this time of year, I've been worried about my SPIRIT DOLL... I'm Afraid its Going to LIVE:

Arlinka is an other-worldly person, like a force of nature. I met her at the first We Folk of Cloth doll conference in the late Nineties. There was a small group of oddball doll makers (us) when most cloth dolls were still cute and blonde. The Soft Sculpture movement that started with Lenore Davis and the Art Quilt movement in the Sixties gave us all permission to work outside the box of beauty and traditional roles, and to push boundaries of materials, imagination, and acceptability.

One can see the power for growth and change in these dolls.

Collecting Personal Symbols: Paper Collage, Journals

Collage journal to collect my personal symbols: Cut 8.5x11" sheets of cardboard, collage, punch holes, and attach with ribbon.

A more emotional collage with images of my mother, me, an ancestor, writing/ranting

For me, writing is as much a part of my art work as sewing or drawing. Even the addition of one word or a quote to a doll can add a deeper dimension of meaning. I know that not everyone writes as much as I do, so I will offer alternatives. You may already be familiar with journaling, rubber-stamping, or scrapbooking. The fact that these techniques are common will make it easier to use them to go deeper.

You or your client may not have time to make a doll or a fabric journal—or this may seem intimidating at first. Starting a paper collection of images, symbols, colors, words, Xerox copies of photos that speak to you is a less threatening way to get into the topics for Transformation. Paper dolls are quicker alternatives to cloth dolls.

As Carl Jung and others have proposed, there are certain colors, shapes, facial expressions, concepts that are universal. In studies across countries and cultures people agree on what they represent. Despite the numerous books on formulaic dream symbols, I think we each develop our own personal symbols based on our life experience, too: colors we wear and use, lucky numbers, or numbers that remind us of an old home, shapes or textures that we find more appealing than others, words of affirmation that make our hearts sing, or chiding phrases that make us feel small. Images or setting that reoccur in our dreams.

I have several different notebooks I keep with inspirations for future projects. A loose-leaf binder works well for collecting Transformative images, either in plastic sleeves or pages with large envelopes attached.

Create dividers by colors, topics, aspirations, projects to address. Transformation does not have to be about disturbing topics—could be vacation plans, inspiration for new work, a healthier body. A binder is good for its flexibility in adding pages and changing emphasis.

SIMPLE JOURNAL: tear 5 sheets of copy paper in half, creating ten 8.5 x 5.5" sheets, stack and fold in half to create a 4.25 x 5.5" book. Use an awl to poke holes in the fold and sew together. I used fine red wire and sewed a stick for the spine. Use clear Acrylic Gel Medium or a glue stick to attach images and words torn from magazines. A glue stick is less messy and doesn't buckle the paper. You could also take an inexpensive book from a thrift store and paint the pages with gesso to make a background for your own personal Transformative journal.

Another ice breaker for writing is to keep a Dream Journal—paper and a pen by the bed to wake up and write down whatever you remember of dreams. Avoiding Censoring is the biggest challenge. Transformative Journals can be used to record ideas for new work when there isn't time to start. To arrange uncensored collections of images and phrases collected without thinking. Your book will not look like anyone else's book—we are individuals. This should not be an art or beauty contest. This journal can be as straight forward or as fancy as you like. Keep it private, if you want to feel more free in your expression. Glue envelopes to the pages and put frightening thoughts into the envelopes for your eyes only.

Above is the simple torn paper journal with a stick spine and the signatures (groups of pages) sewn to a stick.

Below is a pocket fabric journal I made for a Round Robin entitled Stories my Mother Told Me. Styrofoam inside the front and back cover makes a rigid folder. Fabric pages can be sewn inside.

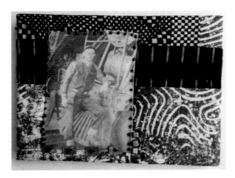

Young Phil

2014 5″ Printable fabric makes small gift collages for my niece & nephew

Happy Wedding

2002 10″ Collage to celebrate Cate and Charley, sketches and program from the wedding.

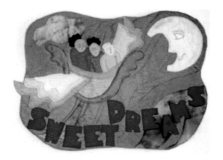

Sweet Dreams

Felt is easy to collage because the edges don't fray. Stitch or just glue.

Topics for a Transformative Journal

Cutting (or tearing) and pasting is SO relaxing! Collect a pile of old magazines and without thinking too much, start ripping out pictures, phrases, fragments of pictures, textures, colors that appeal to you for no reason at all. Don't think. Then sort by type:

TEXTURES: Pleasant-Unpleasant, Hard-Soft, Old-New, Good-Bad. Rough-Smooth.

COLORS: Ones I love-Ones I hate, Ones that are soothing-Ones that are stressing, Ones that are angry-Ones that are Happy-Ones that are sad. Ones that are gentle-Ones that are powerful.

WORDS, PHRASES TO LIVE BY: Your daily Mantra. Mine is: Enough money, Enough time, Enough opportunities. Or the messages you may hear when you try something new: "not good enough, not strong enough, not smart enough." Or the dreaded Shoulds: Should be cleaning, cooking, caring for family. Should be thin, should be quiet, should dress like a model.

INSPIRATIONAL PEOPLE: Heroines and heroes, old and contemporary, mythological, famous, and known only to you.

THINGS I'D LIKE TO POSSESS: Either concrete, like furniture or fast cars or attributes like fame, patience, or wisdom.

PLACES: Where I'd like to be: warm or mountainous or times in history that resonate, like ancient Egypt, modern Paris, the desert, land of fairies and elves, American Frontier.

THINGS, EVENTS, PEOPLE, ANIMALS, SYMBOLS THAT FRIGHTEN ME—OR GIVE ME HOPE AND JOY: Snakes, fire, drowning, explosions, vampires, starvation, Hitler, or Blue sky, rainbow, babies, sunshine, piles of cash, delicious food, fabric.

THINGS/PEOPLE I LOVE: may be same as above or more specific—how about a Transformative Journal celebrating YOU!

FORBIDDEN PLEASURES: Only you know what these are for you.

A POCKET FOR THE PAST: Our ancestors, our triumphs and mistakes, and all the things that create the format for our stories.

A POCKET FOR DREAMS: Be as outrageous as you can. If you don't dream it, you won't do it. If you can't find a picture that symbolizes your image, write phrases that represent your oldest, deepest, most impossible dreams.

THINGS FOR WHICH I WOULD LIKE TO FORGIVE MYSELF: Use symbols or phrases written on scraps of paper. We all beat on ourselves too much. That angst wastes valuable time.

THINGS FOR WHICH I WOULD LIKE TO FORGIVE OTHERS: Events or lack of action that took place recently or deep in the past: my abusive ex-husband, my imperfect parents, a teacher who discouraged me. If you're not yet ready to forgive, it's OK—understanding may help you let go.

MY OWN PERSONAL SYMBOLS: Lucky numbers, a patch from a meaningful garment, a goddess or hero with whom you identify, forms that show up frequently in your work (stars and spirals for me).

SYMBOLS FROM OTHER TIMES AND CULTURES: Working intuitively, pick what resonates with you, remember Carl Jung who teaches the universal meanings of symbols.

Invent your own categories. This format can be used for dealing with traumas, bullying, family tragedies. I find it helpful to choose words or phrases to go with the images and make the thrust more personal.

If you have time, create your Transformtive Journal in fabric. Use *Wonder Under* to steam the images to the backing. Fabrico pens are permanent on fabric or use a running stitch for line.

2004 Letter beads for a self-affirmation series: fabric, beads, found objects, rusty can top.

Happy Fabric Collage
2014 5″ My young parents in 1945.

Yukio Seppuku
1983 Part of the series to leave my marriage.

Linda and Opie O'Brien: Transformative History

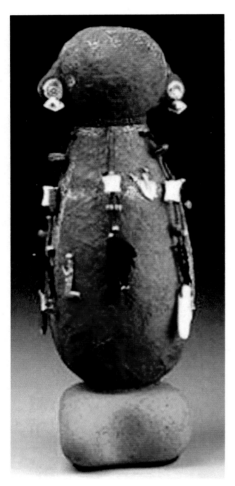

Minikisi
Linda O'Brien

Pillow Doll
Linda O'Brien

Linda and Opie O'Brien:

"Your interest in healing dolls—once upon a time I was very ill—a long story that I will not go into tonight. When I became a reiki master, my path was to create healing vessels filled with healing herbs I grew, chakra stones and positive reiki energy that emanated out to anyone in the vicinity of the vessel. Instead of working directly with people as a naturopath, I was able to combine my passion for organic materials with my artwork and love of rituals, totems and fetish statues. That's how my 'minikisi' dolls came into being. They are based on African totemic power figures usually used for healing. Inside, They are filled with several herbs and many other things, and on the exterior this one proudly wears her medicine bundles over the nails embedded in her. For the various healing petitions...the Minikisi are embellished with milagros and prayer beads, of healing vessels which eventually evolved into healing dolls, because to me dolls are very special and rich in symbolism. And these vessels and dolls would just continually release healing energy to everyone who came into their space.

"I have always had a strong belief in various healing arts and also believe there are many paths leading to an ultimate goal. After I completed my reiki studies, I had difficulty with hands-on, one-on-one sessions and felt it was not my 'path.' My personal belief is that all healing comes from God and I could not charge a fee on a session basis, although many people do, and that's fine, for that is their path. I strongly believe that this positive, universal reiki energy was meant to be shared openly and with anyone, whether they believed in it or not. As an artist I was drawn to create special art pieces, empowered with reiki energy, semi-precious stones, and various healing herbs, which as a naturopath, I grew and dried myself.

These became a series of healing vessels which eventually evolved into healing dolls, because dolls to me are very special and rich in symbolism—and these vessels and dolls would just continually release this healing energy to everyone who came into their space."

Sula Box
Linda O'Brien

Lake Spirit Mask
O'Brien

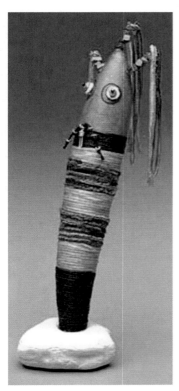

Nana
Linda O'Brien

Gourd Doll
Linda O'Brien

Shield Doll
O'Brien

Riva Weinstein: Transformative History

Riva Weinstein:

Wrapped Barbie
Riva Weinstein Dryer lint and thread.

"My first series of art dolls was called The Goddessey. They were inspired by Cycladian figures I had seen at the Getty museum in Los Angeles when I was writing Barbie(TM) commercials for an advertising agency. I didn't actually make the dolls until many years later and the process unraveled surprising self-discoveries.

"First of all, I realized I had been drawing goddess figures since I was in my teens. Wrapping the dolls in recycled fibers (also known as dryer lint) became a somewhat obsessive act. And in the process I realized that as I was wrapping the dolls, I was unwrapping myself. Re-covering an idealized plastic figure in soft swaddling was self-nurturing. I'd carried this idea around in my head for a long time, so seeing myself complete it was self-actualizing. I was coming home to myself.

"Whether I am wrapping thrift store dolls in fiber or covering medicine and beauty bottles in fiber, wax and clay, making these sacred dolls connects me with an ancient archetype of woman as healer, nurturer, creator. I see this goddess figure everywhere—in boulders by a riverside, in the shape of a cast-off cork screw.

"Doing this kind of work has connected me with other artists like Pamela, whose use of materials and life experience are so inspiring. Some people see my dolls and think they look like mummies, so they think I am making some kind of negative statement, when in fact I am doing exactly the opposite. Artists are often much more aware of the spiritual aspect of the mummy form in relation to transformation and immortality, so they intuitively understand the nature of the figures, or, like Pamela, they are so amused and delighted, they instantly connect with the simple joy of the discovery and laugh wholeheartedly out loud. In the modern world products inspire so much worship. Medicine and beauty are often viewed as both our physical and our spiritual salvations."

"I often think about how one can practice one's art in these corporate environments, in ways that will initiate change, but not instigate trouble. Corporate environments (like dojo floors) do not encourage nails sticking up out of the floor - a reference to an old Japanese saying. How does one create subversions that make their point without creating unnecessary drama?"

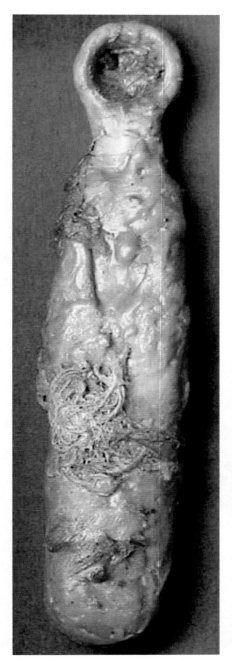

Wax Doll

Riva Weinstein:

"Last night I drew Artemis - the mistress of animals, and wild untamed things. She is a symbol of independence. A reminder of the value of solitude and a path to healing through fear. This morning I drew Tlazolteot. She is a Toltec earth mother, and like Kali embodies both the creative and devouring. The last line of the card reads: She is proof that anything that can overwhelm and destroy us also has the power to heal and grant forgiveness.

"Today, that is my lifeline, as I offer my distress a nurturing cup of tea, asking what flavor it would like, embracing it in the winged arms of my spirit guide, whose legs are the roots of earth and whose body and mind reach into the endless expanse of sky."

Riva Weinstein is a Hudson Valley and NYC artist and writer. I caught up with her blog: http://www.magic-medicine-workshop.blogspot.com/ where she hasn't posted frequently, but was working on a masters degree, back at a job in NYC, demonstrating for recycling, and writing up a storm.

All-Purpose Icons, Paper and Fabric

A lot can be expressed in a simple shape in fabric. The two-piece (front and back) type of pattern is the simplest to make, but can be very expressive in the kind of fabric you use and the way it is embellished. You may buy my: Pamela's Designing A Doll and Making Faces Book, if you want step by step instruction on how I make my more complicated forms.

Icons are simple forms that represent larger ideas. Their use has grown tremendously with the expansion of technology in the ten years since I first wrote this book. Usually people in the culture that creates the icon share an understanding of what it means. Icons were used to signify religious figures eons before writing and computers were invented. As Carl Jung has observed, similar forms often show up in disparate cultures and places. Simple forms are powerful vehicles for story and magic.

Make the Icon personal to you, with your colors and symbols, attach a fortune, embellish. Create a face with very simple lines, with a collage of a photo of you, or no face. Punch holes and attach limbs with brads. You can change the body expression by how you arrange the limbs. Very simple face lines and re-arrangement of arms and legs change the mood.

Because the Icon shapes are simple, they can be done in paper or fabric. Paper dolls and very simple dolls with pre-sewn bodies are easier to use in short-term groups. Stitch any of the icons from two layers of unbleached muslin, sew on the traced line, leaving an opening along a straight edge, turn, stuff, slip stitch the opening closed and use markers, ribbons, beads for embellishing. I LOVE piecing, and often sew small pieces of fabric together, then draw and sew my icon bodies.

Put an affirmation inside the doll with the stuffing or paste it to the back of the paper doll. The affirmation can result from a timed period of stream-of-consciousness writing.

My Personal Symbols

2003 Moon, stars, Sun, French Fortune, mask face, red. There would be more red and spirals if I did my symbols today.

Paper All-Purpose Icon

Pattern on next page. Follow directions on the pattern. Use brads when attaching the body parts using paper. You could also trace around the body parts on two layers of fabric, seam, turn, stuff, attach limbs with buttons.

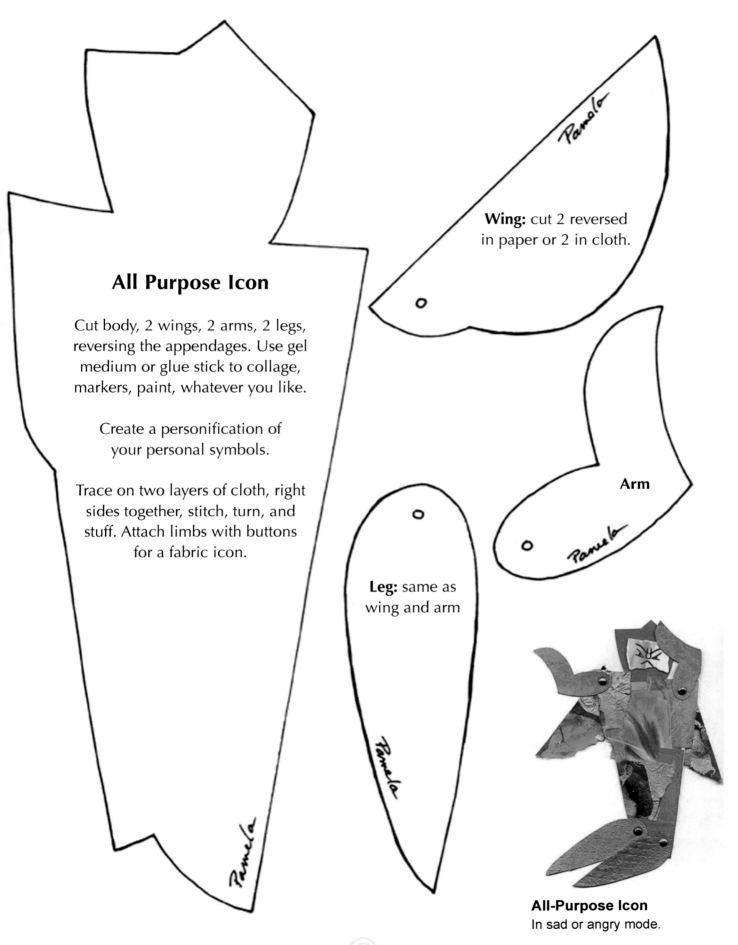

All Purpose Icon

Cut body, 2 wings, 2 arms, 2 legs, reversing the appendages. Use gel medium or glue stick to collage, markers, paint, whatever you like.

Create a personification of your personal symbols.

Trace on two layers of cloth, right sides together, stitch, turn, and stuff. Attach limbs with buttons for a fabric icon.

Wing: cut 2 reversed in paper or 2 in cloth.

Arm

Leg: same as wing and arm

All-Purpose Icon
In sad or angry mode.

Transforming the Self

*"Out beyond ideas of Wrong-Doing and Right-Doing, there is a field.
I'll meet you there."*
— Rumi

Always More
2003 15″ Tin box body, fabric and
mixed media—my philosophy of life.

Melancholy
2014 12″ I've added wall pieces to
my repertoire for expressing feeling
and family history—seeing, writing,
making helps with resolution.

So many choices in life! I've learned that just because I'm good at something or can make money at it doesn't mean that I have to follow that path. And just because I don't know how to do it now doesn't mean that I can't learn. It appears to me that I've known all along what I need to do with my life, but the "should" messages get in the way, the fear messages, not to mention the overpowering necessity for food/clothing/shelter, and I've only been actually able to do my art life in pieces of time won from my other responsibilities. Like most people.

Life/survival for ordinary folk seems to be more and more of a struggle since I wrote the first version of this book. Now my life is All Art, All the Time, but I earned that freedom with 25 years of working in health care and lots of careful saving.

Learning to listen to your inner voice , inner "knowing" is so simple, yet so challenging to trust! "Follow your intuition."
How many times we've heard that, and how hard it is to do!

Please give yourself permission to follow your own personal dream in whatever ways you are able each moment. You probably do have a sense of what your dream is: think back to what you wanted to do/be at five or seven or twelve. Of course I wanted to be a cowgirl or actress and have changed my mind about that, but there is an element of my dreams in how I organize, lead, and inspire my students.

What did you enjoy playing with? I was writing and illustrating books by five, directing plays, telling my four younger brothers and anyone else who would listen what to do and how to do it. It's a lifetime journey, so at times you'll make great strides and sometimes baby steps.

Give yourself permission to be successful at what you love. Don't sabotage your own efforts by always putting others' needs ahead of you own—or cleaning the house before your true work. We can't truly care for others if we don't care for ourselves first. Differentiate your efforts from those of others by being true to yourself, building a monument to your own uniqueness.

"The real goal is a vocation that feels like a vacation," says Carol Armitage, my SCORE advisor. My mother grew up during the Depression and has never succeeded in feeling as if she has Enough security. She pushed me to learn the trade of Occupational Therapy in college, so I would never be dependent on a man for security. I worked two years and quit to make a living doing craft shows for twenty-five years. Then, giving into my fears of ending up a bag lady, I spent over ten years working my way up through the medical hierarchy again, making plenty of money, building a house, saving up a nest egg, and looking for a job I could love in health care, where I knew management and regulations backward and forward. I had tried to get the company I was working for to pay attention to my ideas, so I could feel proud to work there. I tried working for a data management company that was too reminiscent of my relationship with my abusive ex-husband. All Art, All the Time is my true vocation.

The only viable career for me seemed to be to follow my heart into art, teaching, writing. The Universe was telling me what to do, but it took me a long time and lots of coaching to pay attention, and I ended up having to go back to OT one last time for almost ten years when I took myself to the West Coast.

You may not need to go into business for yourself, but when you make a concrete vision of whatever you want to achieve, you are more likely to succeed. "I am an artist." "I deserve respect in my relationships." I will follow at least one aspect of my dream, even if it takes a long time." Both times I returned to health care, I had to wear the lab coat and STUDY LIKE MAD to convince myself I could be successful, so I could convince my patients, the doctors, and the staff I supervised that I was competent. The part of me that did the best in that job was the teacher/counselor/leader part. Some days I was comfortable in the lab coat...and I became a very good splint maker...sculpture and my ability to see in three dimensions and translate flat materials to round. I see how much I have continued to evolve into who I really am over the subsequent ten years since I moved West because I felt that this was where I needed to be. I entered health care for one last time, because I knew I would need the money I could save there. I met so many wonderful people and helped them to heal and traded stories and encouraged them to follow their own dreams in whatever way they could.

She Did Her Best
2014 24" Mixed media, painting and collage—working intuitively from a photo of Mom and me, still resolving feelings.

Where?
2014 11" I drove across the US and back in 2014, looking for where I belong physically and emotionally. I used objects I collected on my trip for this piece: the arch from MI, the silk cocoon from VT, the petrified wood from ND, and the image from the road.

Now I am again re-creating my life-long concurrent picture of myself as an artist/writer/transformation facilitator, dressed in paint-stained jeans and layered sweat shirts for work and bright hand-made clothes for public appearances.

Grow your internal picture of your Self, through what you have accomplished, what you would like to be, all the good things you really are. There are no wrong answers. There is great beauty in every effort. As much as you can, be In The Moment, without judgement but with wide open eyes and heart. Be reborn as a child with that innocence and lack of a preconceived notion of what the outcome should be.

Art Pamela

Rehab Director Pamela

Be open to whatever comes out, live with it to see what emerges. It is good to do this within the safety and support of a trusted group and within a comfortable medium like doll making, which you'll see is a safe way to explore grand ideas and dreams as well as anger, sadness, and parts of yourself that might be socially unacceptable if magnified and expressed more overtly.

While working with doll making in a Transformative way you can discover and hone your own Life's Purpose, as well as making friends with your own True Self. As you stitch and delve and spend time with your ideas and feelings, the truth of who you are and want to be will become more clear.

Emerging: Symbol of Transformation

Emerging was a way to work with the feelings associated with growing into my Self and my fuller ability to use my skills and who I am, Neitzsche's "Whatever doesn't kill me makes me stronger." Living with and escaping from my abusive husband made me stronger and more sympathetic to others in that position. Being poor made me realize I could survive. Working in health care taught me a lot about organization and selling and being able to talk to a wide variety of people.

The animal skull in Emerging came from the field that my studio looked out onto. Skulls carry lots of symbolism: mortality, the structure under the skin, or the kind of joyful celebration mixed with sadness from Mexico's Day of the Dead sugar skulls. I collect skulls and this one sat on my work table for years while I tried to figure out what to do with it.

I allow the forces of chance to assist me, knowing that I am making choices, even when it doesn't appear to be so. When I need something, it shows up, but because on some level I was looking for it. I did sketches and waited, finding the carved face at the bead store in Woodstock, NY. Then I took a construction class from Lois Schklar http://www.loisschklar.com/ She gave us permission to use Any connection technique that worked. I pass that permission on to you. That really got me moving. I used aluminum foil, WeldBond, and armature, and the figure started to take shape. She reminded me of something emerging from a shell or chrysalis.

Through the process of working on this figure I decided to quit health care for the second time, for something that was more fitting to my true nature. Then to leave the house and relationship where I built the figure. None of that was in my mind when I started, but I Emerged.

Emerging
2003 14″ Symbol of growing into my self.

Self-Transformation

What living, thinking person doesn't want to transform her/him self at times? The first project, putting the journal together, was a way to pick and choose without thinking too much and start to see a pattern of the symbols and issues that are closest to your heart. Working on a Transformative doll or project is a way to focus your energy on an area or areas that you would like to change within yourself, but also to learn to accept and cherish aspects of yourself that may not match the mainstream idea of what a perfect woman or perfect person might be.

Perhaps because I am female, I see in advertising how we are supposed to be young, thin, and beautiful in a Caucasian, Barbie doll sort of way: kind, good, and always pleasant, helpful to those around us. I'll tell you right now, I'm not any of those things consistently, and in addition, I'm slightly overweight, wrinkled, selfish, and downright insecure and bitchy at times. I have some good qualities, too, one of which is my constant effort to be honest.

Part of the ongoing Transformative process is learning to know and love all of our many parts. By knowing and accepting our own lacks of perfection, we can also more easily accept those deficiencies in others.

In 1991, the fist time I had to go back to OT I got a job in a hospital. I had to make up for what I didn't learn in school, what had changed; and I lived in fear of inadvertently hurting someone. That dread plagued me again when I returned to OT in 2004. I also felt like a total failure at the art work I really wanted to do, because I couldn't make a reliable living. Each night I came home and walked by the frozen Hudson River, wondering how long it would take to die among the ice floes. Some spark of determination—or fear of the cold water—kept me going, and I made a conscious decision that if I were going to have to do this work, I might as well find things about it to enjoy, and something interesting about each patient.

Crochet Guy
2000-2005 8-12" tall. When I travel or especially when I visit my mother, I need to have something to do with my hands, so I crochet free-form figures. It's amazing how different their personalities can be! I use Crayola Model Magic to make faces, coloring them with any kind of acrylic paint. The body becomes a blank canvas on which to play and explore to see what comes out. This is definitely a male, with his dangling amber appendage and rusty nail (another phallic symbol) on his chest. In spite of his armor, he doesn't look all that sure of himself.

Birdwoman
2012 12" Quilted, beads, sequins. For flying away from trouble

I recommend finding thing to like about what one has to do. I did love the regular pay checks, the mastery of new skills, the concrete appreciation of my efforts through patients going home healed, meeting interesting people, and raises based on my efforts.

I saw an endless stream of little old ladies with wrist fractures and people on Workers' Compensation, some of whom didn't appear to be quite honest about the severity of their injury or whose neediness seemed to be exacerbated by their injury. I determined to learn something new and find something to enjoy from each patient. I only failed with one man, who seemed so intent on abusing everyone in sight that he finally succeeded in making me angry, too. But we did triumph by sending him home at last. There are always things to be learned no matter how bad the situation may seem at first. I continue to have nightmares about being responsible for endless rows of people in wheelchairs. I left health care for good at the end of 2013. I met wonderful people, heard great stories, and did some good work, even though it was not a profession to which I was naturally suited. I learned business and leadership skills and an ability to separate my self-worth from the sometimes narrow views of others.

I still plan to work with healing and self-healing through the use of art, though I can't make any concrete claims beyond: try it and see how you feel. I may be working locally with a social worker friend with cancer sufferers. I just heard a quote from NPR that one in three women and one in two men in the US will have a diagnosis of cancer before they die. There is also the looming question for us Baby Boomers of the effects of life and aging, from which there is no recovery. But we do have choices about how we manage the passage. From working in Palliative Care, I recognize that Western culture is habituated to ignoring aging and death. We and our families need to start paying attention and treat this phase of life with dignity and maybe joy. We can only look youthful for so long and aging is going to start affecting a larger and larger portion of our population. The realities of life are different from the advertised ideals of life. Transformative doll making can help us resolve the discrepancies.

Creativity
2005 8″ Stick Doll

Love Yourself
2010 16″ I adapted my Hot Flash pattern for a heart disease campaign geared toward Women and taking care of our hearts

Transformative Paper Dolls

Paper dolls are a perfect medium for Transformation, especially if you don't have a lot of time or money. When working with a group, pre-cut the bodies. This paper doll is double-sided with a different mood or personality on the back. One of the things I gained from working with a Personal Coach before I left NY was a heightened awareness of the power of language, especially Self Talk. I had been describing my inherited tendency toward depression as manic/depressive. Tessa taught me to re-label Bright and Dark Days, or moments. It seems a kinder way of describing myself and makes managing the moods easier.

How would a paper doll of you look on one of your dark versus one of your bright days? What things/colors/words/images symbolically weigh you down on a dark day? How can you express this using simple forms and papers? Using a copy of your face in happy and sad moods, make a double-sided self-portrait. See how easy it can be to flip the mood. The process of making a doll can help to solidify a new view of yourself.

All-Purpose Paper Doll
2007 10" Self-portrait with positive affirmations

Happy Flash
2004 18" Wall hanging puts a positive spin on menopause.

Wider is Better Paper Doll
2009 13" Celebrates what you can't change, in the brightest, happiest colors.

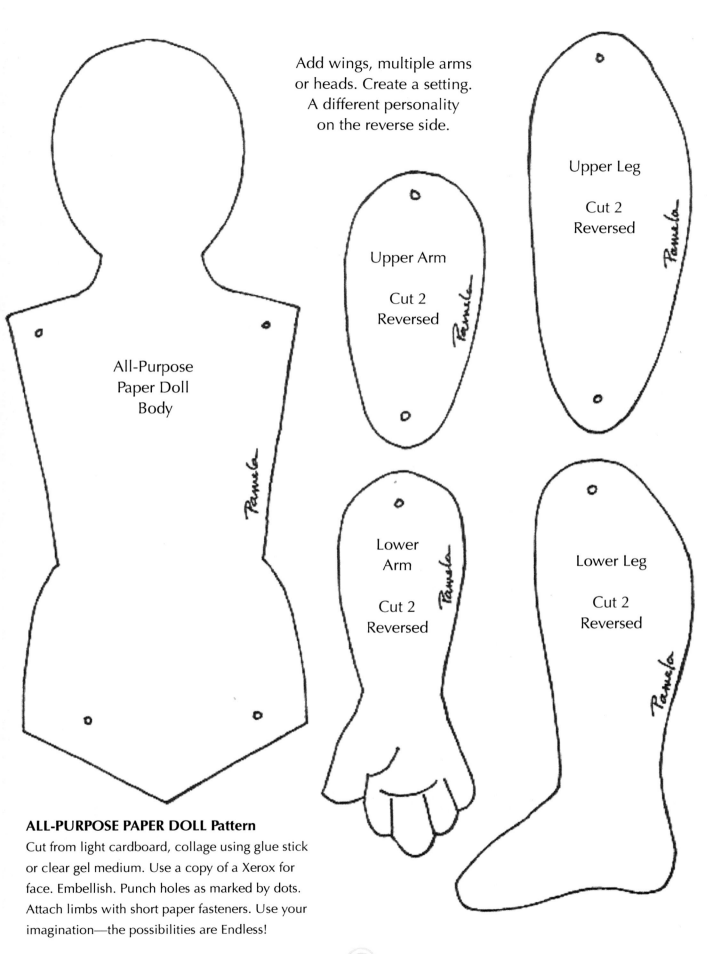

Add wings, multiple arms or heads. Create a setting. A different personality on the reverse side.

Upper Leg

Cut 2
Reversed

Upper Arm

Cut 2
Reversed

All-Purpose
Paper Doll
Body

Lower
Arm

Cut 2
Reversed

Lower Leg

Cut 2
Reversed

ALL-PURPOSE PAPER DOLL Pattern

Cut from light cardboard, collage using glue stick or clear gel medium. Use a copy of a Xerox for face. Embellish. Punch holes as marked by dots. Attach limbs with short paper fasteners. Use your imagination—the possibilities are Endless!

Eileen McGarvey: Changing People and Circumstances

I have known Eileen McGarvey for a number of years, although I've never met her in person. She is a talented artist who supports herself and her husband by supervising girls with mental health and addiction issues. She uses her art effectively to work with some of the emotional baggage that accompanies these troubled teens.

Eileen uses a variety of media: felting, beading, dolls, vinyl dolls, two-dimensional images and words in journals. She is currently working on a project about an artist friend who died in 2015, and she is helping me by editing this book.

Beaded Meat Doll with Red Dancing Shoes
Eileen McGarvey Three-dimensional beaded doll about women who persevere in spite of our culture.

Damaged Goods (Above and Below)
About the girls with whom Eileen has worked.

Brabbit
Sharpie-colored vinyl form.

Hot Flash Women: Working to Embrace what we Can't Change

I started making Hot Flash Women dolls before I had any personal experience with the term. From the very beginning, the concept just seemed another excuse to put women down and try to make us ashamed of our selves/our bodies. I produced HOT FLASH! A Celebration in 2010 and taught online Hot Flash classes, as always, using dolls and other forms of art making to help negotiate the twists and turns of this potentially traumatic passage. Now that I and many of my friends are retired from regular jobs, the whole issue of aging, losing powers, facing change and eventual death are becoming part of the issues that we can address with doll making. What is the meaning and import of our lives to date and our future lives?

promote what you love instead of bashing what you hate

Eileen:

"I think a lot. I have brilliant ideas (well, according to me, lol) I start a lot of things, but sometimes I think just thinking about things is enough. It's the fun part and very satisfying. But I am learning (again) that doing, while it may not be the instant gratification of ideas, teaches in a whole different way. It is like the difference between a quick snack and a deeply satisfying meal. It teaches me about me and fear, persistence, frustration—and getting to the other side."

Promote what You Love Instead of Bashing What You Hate

Eileen McGarvey Paper doll, with hot flash journal (**below**). I got to know Eileen through her participation in several of my classes and now being in touch on FaceBook. Do a Yahoo Search on Eileen McGarvey Dolls for more.

Paper doll from the online Hot Flash Group. Eileen is able to work creatively in many media.

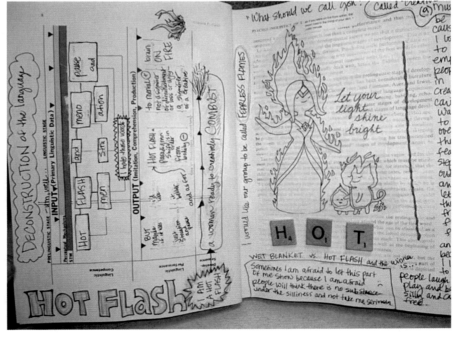

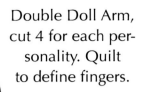

Double Doll Arm, cut 4 for each personality. Quilt to define fingers.

DOUBLE DOLL PATTERN
Cut 2 bodied, reversing on the dotted line, or cutting each end a different color or pattern and seaming on the dotted line. Sew, turn, stuff, leaving an opening on a straight side.

Fold here and make the other end a mirror image

Make a skirt long enough to cover the head on the opposite side, with fabric to match the body on each side.

Be as elaborate as you want with embellishment and facial expression.

Attach appropriately colored arms to shoulders on each side.

The meditative process of stitching, beading, or collecting and pasting bits of paper allows us to dwell on issues that lie just below the conscious level. This may be a very long process, spanning weeks, months, years, and there are always new ramifications to discover. I find working in the abstract helpful in that it allows me to express myself freely, rather than being distracted by struggling to achieve realism.

I have had a life-long dialog with myself about my relationship with art, and its relationship with me. The drive to make art is sometimes difficult to explain or fit into a "normal" life. My Queen of the May series was inspired partly by my first encounter with batiks in the early Nineties at a quilt store in the Amana Colonies in Iowa, where everyone in the shop knew and laughed about addiction to fabric accumulation. The hand-dyed ribbon came from a traditional doll show in Santa Fe.

I had the materials on my work table and tried to just start working without planning out the process. The Queen of the May is my sometimes silly or frivolous public self, with my creative muse as the Darker Self where I let all my anger and fears be present, the aspect of me that is not always socially-acceptable, but is still a vital part of me. The dark feelings can be safely expressed through doll making: the Queen of the May first Ignores, Confronts, Embraces her Darker Self, then the Darker Self becomes almost a pet with the two matured and working together, in the last piece: the Queen of the May and her Familiar.

Preparing for your own project: go to a private and quiet place with your transformative journal. Close your eyes and leave your mind open to meditation on your past, Present, or future. There may be an issue that has been bothering you for years or an uncomfortable event that happened today at work. You may be planning a big life change, from marriage to retirement to moving. Open your eyes and jot down all the words that come into your mind, then the associated colors, shapes, textures. Make a line down the center of a page, with the pros on one side, the cons on the other, with the associations they create in your mind, Mind Mapping

Finished Double Doll
Endless possibilities-duality!

Queen of the May and Her Darker Self One
1998 11″ My first batiks, hand-dyed ribbon, bone faces. First couple in the series set the tone.

Queen of the May Ignores Her Darker Self II
1998 12″ More elaborate.

Queen of the May and Her Familiar
2003 13″ After I moved to WA. Friendlier, Model Magic face.

Rosie Maxine Chapman: Transforming History

Rosie:

Problem Solver
Rosie Maxine   Black Barkcloth

Portrait Quilt of Howllin Wolf
Rosie Maxine

"I was a Tom Boy. Never wanted to do girly things, like play with dolls, comb the dolls' hair, or talk to dolls. At the ripe old age of 43, that all changed.

"For years I knew I had to have a hysterectomy and just kept putting it off. Finally my beloved fibroid became so huge that people started asking me when the baby was due! Well, I sort of thought to myself, 'Hmmmm, maybe it's time for a hysterectomy!' As we have all been told, hysterectomies are no big deal, fibroid tumors are non cancerous—a walk-in-the-park surgery, right? WRONG! After eight painful months of Lupron shots to reduce the huge fibroid tumor (to no avail, of course) I had the procedure. Ten days later, the doctor calls and tells me she thinks the tumor was malignant. Boy, was I angry!!!!!! Okay, so I went to see the oncologist/gynecologist who performed a second surgery four weeks after the first surgery in order to remove the remaining female organs as well as lymph nodes and my appendix—No Problem!

"I knew God was just testing me, so I dealt with it. When I returned to my fun job at the maximum-security facility for juvenile delinquent boys less than two months later, I was still in pain. That was October 1992. In February 1993 three teens decided they were going to escape from the facility by throwing me down the stairs while I was transporting eighteen boys to the lower level of the building. I landed on my back and after being unconscious for a few seconds, radioed for help and bravely escorted the three culprits back to their rooms.

"Needless to say, I ended up at home with severe back and neck pains as well as a feeling of being in shock. It took about three weeks for the post-traumatic stress disorder to kick in , and when it did, I went into a deep depression, rarely left the house alone except to see the oncologist, psychologist, and physical therapist. And I sat in the dark for about five months.

"Prior to the accident I had applied to return to graduate school to work on a combined masters and PhD in clinical psychology.

"In July of that year my sister Barb brought over a doll she had just purchased. I took one look at the doll and I said to myself, 'I can make a doll better than that!' so I called up a friend's daughter to go with me to Jo-Ann Fabrics to buy a doll pattern. Lo and Behold, I found just what I needed, a Raggedy Ann doll pattern!

I made about fifteen African-American Raggedy Ann and Andy dolls and put them in a small frame shop a month later, where they sold like hot cakes. I was accepted into the University of Michigan's School of Social Work Master's program, but had no job or money to pay for school. Thank God for financial aid!

"After four months of making the rag dolls I wanted a new challenge, so I read several doll magazines and discovered the world of art dolls and sculpting life-like figures. I then began sculpting and selling polymer clay sculpted old Black men and women as well as Black clowns. After almost two years of being afraid of the dark, sleeping less than three hours a night, and feeling lost, I became alive again. The dolls were my saving grace throughout those dark days and lonely nights. I told no one what I was doing through because I really didn't understand it myself. The psychologist was no help. Because I refused to take any mood-altering prescribed drugs my medical insurance was eliminated. Because I refused to go back to work at the lock-up, I was fired from my job. But I pressed onward and upward and continued to create the most magnificent dolls I had ever seen. Looking back they weren't all that magnificent, but because I had never had art and was self-taught, I thought I was too tough for words."

Early in her doll making career Rosie recognized that people love dolls that look like them. We are not all blonde Barbies. Dolls celebrate our uniqueness. Rosie continues to do Story Telling, Social Work, and Political Consciousness-Raising in the Midwest and on FaceBook.

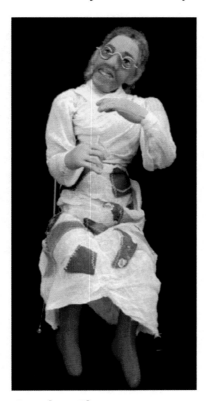

Grandma Clara
Rosie Maxine Cotton, Fimo

Kool Kid Keisha
Rosie Maxine Cotton

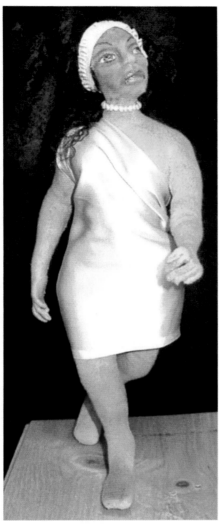

Runway Model
Rosie Maxine This doll reflects Rosie's improved Self-Image.

"Dolls have been my art therapy. They have transformed this 'rag doll' broken in spirit, at one time a physical and emotional wreck of a being to an artist. The art dolls I have created in the past ten years (written in 2003) are in homes all over the world. My sideline career as a story teller taps into my theatrical background. By day I am a school social worker in an alternative school, a grade school, and a junior high school. I use my own experiences to help at-risk and special-needs students. Currently I am working toward another master's degree. This time it will be in art therapy because I know the power that art has on the healing process."

I caught up with Rosie Maxine again recently on Facebook, where she mentioned creating fabric postcards and encouraging others to make and send them in honor of Black History Month. Story telling and doll making both help spread the message of empowerment and improvement. Rosie is helping others in every aspect of her life. She earned another Masters in 2012. in Art Education with a concentration in Art Therapy. She continues to perform as a storyteller and works as a school social worker and has now added Art Therapist to her resume.

Joyce Bryant
Rosie Maxine Fabric postcard.

Sojourner Truth
Rosie Maxine Fiber postcard.

Rosie Maxine Chapman is now also making Portrait Art Quilts and Fabric postcards in addition to dolls and her job as a school clinical social worker in Michigan. She is also known as Miz Rosie, the story teller for the last twenty years, thrilling audiences of all ages with her interactive story edutrainment.

FABRIC POSTCARDS

Fabric Postcards are just like regular postcards. Use the standard postcard size 4.25" x 6" and ¼" thick for a standard first class stamp. Larger or thicker dimensions will cost more.

Use card stock for stiffening and writing your message on the back. Make the front like a quilt, with images, trim, beading, and embroidery backed with a thin layer of stuffing, then a layer of Pellon or other fabric stiffener. Zigzag stitch the font layers and back card stock together around the edges.

It's best to take the postcard to the post office to be hand cancelled and make sure there's sufficient postage.

Remember Mama
Rosie Maxine

Their Music Lives on!!
Rosie Maxine Postcard

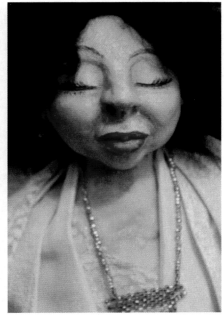

Angel of Return
Rosie Maxine

Dayle Doroshow: Self Transformation

The Wishing Chair
Dayle Doroshow 12" Wood, polymer clay, candles

Dayle:

"I made the Wishing Chair at a time in my life when I was seeking direction and wanted and needed to focus on goals and dreams that truly are important to me. The act of building this 'Altar' was very meditative. The doll is created with polymer clay with this quote printed on the torso: 'NOBODY CAN CONCEIVE OR IMAGINE ALL THE WONDERS THERE ARE UNSEEN AND UNSEEABLE IN THE WORLD.'

"When the Wishing Chair was complete, I created a tiny book containing ALL I HOPE AND STRIVE TO BE."

Dayle Doroshow lives in a magical house in the middle of a grove of redwoods on the coast of California. She uses a variety of materials to create her pieces, simple shapes, usually in environments, and often accompanied by books, which, along with the words on and about the pieces, add even more to the depth of meaning.

She lives near the famous dump by the ocean in Fort Bragg, California, where we picked up many treasures for our mixed media art.
Dayle teaches classes all over the US and leads adventures in France.

CHAIR EXERCISE

Decorate a small chair from Michael's or a doll house as your own personal WISHING CHAIR, using your favorite colors and embellishments.

Make a skeleton with armature wire or re-bar wrapping wire and bend it to sit in the chair. Wrap the armature with strips of some of your favorite fabrics which may be rubber-stamped or inscribed with personal aspirations or symbols from your Transformative Journal. You may collage significant images onto the wrapped body with diluted white glue or acrylic gel medium.

Or sew a very simple shape as a body (as shown) insert armature wire in a loop with ends sticking out of the neck. Stuff around the armature wire. Build a head shape from aluminum foil over the ends of the wire, cover with Crayola Model Magic to build a simple head.

Stuff around the armature wire, making sure that the piece will still "sit", don't stuff too tightly. Use beading and embroidery to decorate the body and form the head around the ends of wire as above. (I used an ArtGirls pewter face).

Keep a piece of paper close by to write thoughts, words, and phrases that flow into your mind as you work. Or you can decorate a small journal to accompany your piece.

Create an altar in your studio with your Wishing Chair. Add symbolic figures and objects to the area. Light a candle to your creativity/happiness/success/whatever.

Use the piece as a reminder to focus your energy on working toward the realization of your goals.

A doll house chair my mother gave me. When I was in high school we collected dolls together. Our tastes have diverged since.

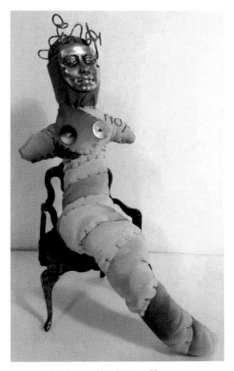

My Wishing Chair Doll
Sits in the chair, but wishes NOT to be my mother

Wrapped Stick Dolls

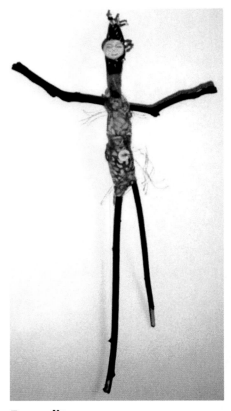

Go outside and gather 6-10 sticks, indigenous and ones that speak to you, six to twelve inches long. Check to be sure they aren't too brittle, because you'll want your creation to last. Empty your mind of expectations and play with different arrangements of the sticks to create a human or animal figure. Use narrow masking tape to hold the sticks in their new relationships. You can break the sticks to fit the vision they suggest, or add more sticks to support a head. Use narrow strips of quilt batting or rags, wrapping to fill out the body form and cover the tape. You can use a hot glue gun, Aileens' Tacky Glue, or stitching with heavy thread to hold the fibers in place. Use scraps of cloth, charms, beads, more stitching as your motif emerges.

If you know what you want this figure to say from the beginning, you can add an affirmation inside the body or write on a strip of wrapping fabric with an indelible pen. If you know the symbolism of herbs and flowers, you can include some very dry plant materials inside the doll. Wet plants might mold or attract bugs.

Fecundity
With protruding belly and message. The recipient soon was expecting a son.

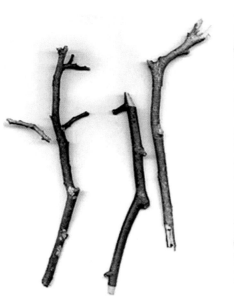

Sticks suggest body shapes, jump-starting the doll

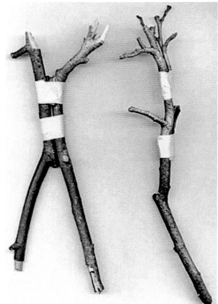

Sticks taped into body shapes

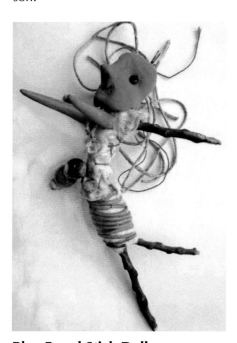

Blue Faced Stick Doll
2013 7" I made this doll with a blue Model Magic face while I was teaching a class. Pointy bead breasts, string hair

Make a head from two pieces of heavy paper glued front and back to one of your sticks, stitching or using beads down the sides. Or wrap the head and sew on a button, bead, or charm, or build a face from Crayola Model Magic (paper clay for kids). When the head is dry, paint it with acrylic paints or sew right through it, using beads to hold it in place. The Blue Faced Wrapped stick Doll on page 52 has a painted Model Magic face.

Getting back to issues to explore with doll making: are there two sides (or more) to your chosen past or future issue? Are there two sides to the current You that you would like to reconcile and integrate, such as Artist and Mom, Conservative and Wild, Past and Future? Make a line down the center of a page and put the pros on one side, the cons on the other, with the colors and images they create in your mind.

For inspiration, look in or add to your Things to Get Rid Of or Things I Like About Myself journal page pockets (p.24). You may find yourself moving images and phrases from one pocket to another throughout these sessions and beyond. Use colors, textures, and images to express your feelings without words. Choose one of your pockets and pull out all of the contents to make a paper doll or wrapped doll of yourself. You may include a door in your Symbolic Self, in head, heart, or belly, that opens to reveal more. Read about chakras to see where in your body different aspects of your self might be expressed.

Save your Transformative Journal...you can come back to it later and see what's changed or improved over time. You may want to add more or different sections in the future.

How is your Relationship with your Self?

What would you like to leave behind or change?

How can you symbolize that?

Finished Stick Dolls
From the stick arrangements on page 52. Heavy paper faces on the right. Bead face on the left.

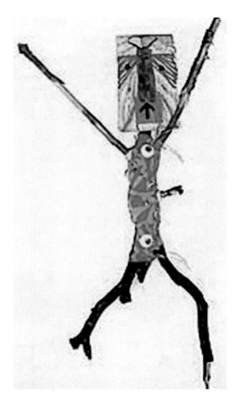

Wrapped Orange Stick Doll
Watercolor paper face

Rosie Rojas: Self-Transformation

"As I sit here writing this and thinking about deadlines I have to make for doll magazines and doll classes that I have to work on and a hundred e-mails that I need to answer, I realize just how much my dolls have transformed my life. How far they have helped lift me from that dark abyss where I stood long ago feeling lost and hopeless. The path out of my depression and the path of my doll making are so intertwined that I am not sure where or if ever they were separate.

"Today my world is full of friends and fellow doll artists that share their lives and ideas with me through my classes and doll clubs and conventions and the Internet. I have a beautiful daughter and a great son-in-law and a new grandson. A husband who is a partner in all my endeavors and loves to travel to doll conventions with me.

"Things weren't always so. To paraphrase Dante, 'In the middle of my life I came upon a dark woods.' I seemed to lose my way in those dark woods and it took me over ten years to find my way out. Shortly after the birth of my daughter I suffered from post partum depression.

"It went undiagnosed and I struggled with this on and off for several years. At about age thirty, when things appeared (at least to the outside) to be going fine, I hit a psychological and spiritual wall. I fell apart, I had hit rock bottom. I quit my job and retreated into my bedroom. I was completely lost in those dark woods. My life had come to a halt. It was a struggle to get from one day to the next. Needless to say, I didn't do much in the way of art at that time.

"Reluctantly, after a year of this I was forced to seek therapy. People who are depressed aren't easy to convince they need help. My pastor referred me to a psychotherapist and thus began a relationship that lasted almost twelve years. During one of my sessions my therapist suggested I try and express some of the emotions I was trying to deal with by using art. I had never been much for painting and drawing, so I thought I'd try and sculpt. First I discovered that working with my hands was soothing, transporting me away from my inner pain. I found amazing faces emerging from the clay, first crude and childlike, then I began to notice their expressions, which only came alive when I began to discuss these emotions with my therapist.

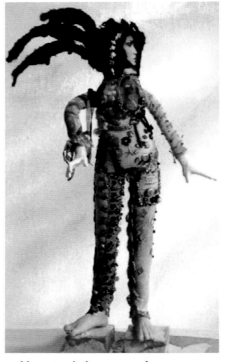

Self Portrait in Mourning
Rosie Rojas

"Eventually, of course, doll making became a passion. I couldn't get enough of it. I read all I could and experimented with every medium I could get my hands on, soon realizing I needed to find teachers to help me. Being an introvert and suffering from depression, this was a huge step out of my world.

"I came upon an ancient soul named May Gene Flatt, a porcelain doll teacher more than willing to share her skills, and more importantly her wonderful outlook on life. I became her eternal student and friend.

"But I wanted to sculpt and found great teachers like Jack Johnston. When I saw an ad for Marlaine Verhelst's doll seminar in France, I informed my husband that I was going. He said, 'Fine.' On the plane to France alone, I panicked and thought to myself, 'What is an introverted depressed woman doing going to France to learn doll making?' My dolls were still leading me, taking me beyond what I thought were my boundaries.

"I met Cyndy Seiving through the Internet, and a crazy bunch of Ohio doll makers called the Guilded Lilies. I soon found a new canvas in fiber-art dolls. I now teach both polymer doll sculpting and fiber art doll making, and my doll making world continues to expand.

"Those who suffer from depression know the pain and anguish this disease can cause. There is a way out. There is medication and therapy, and for me, thankfully, there were my dolls. They were my outlet, my expression, my guides through the dark woods. As I look back at my dolls, I can still feel those emotions that I dealt with at the time, emotions that I can now better understand. But I also see mystery and magic in them. I see so much that I still have to learn from them and each time I begin a new doll, I anxiously await the results."

Hope
Rosie Rojas

Monster Babe
Rosie Rojas

Personal Shrine for Focusing Energy and Intention

Prosperity Shrine
2006 7" Box, bingo card, fimo eye, fortune, punchella, stamp.

Broken, Lost
2006 9" Stick, fabric, belt buckle, shell, charms, sad face on paper, reflecting my mood.

Often we women, have difficulty accepting that good and even wonderful things can happen to us, either through our own efforts or by chance. It can be a bit frightening to enjoy good fortune. Witness the cultures that have rituals to protect new babies from the Evil Eye, from tiger hats and slippers for children to not saying a real name, to the superstitious conviction that any good fortune is easy to lose. We may bear the inherited Calvinist or Catholic idea that we don't "deserve" good fortune. Or the often-inherited idea that we, as women, can't be successful, and if we celebrate our hard-earned good fortune, we will be punished for striving.

I see some of these attitudes slowly, slowly changing during my lifetime. More awareness of sexual preference, race, religious, and class stereotypes. The old class system is constantly being re-built in the US, by the concentration of wealth and access to education and health care into a smaller and smaller group of hands.

I worked my way out of an abusive marriage by replacing the messages my husband heaped on me about my stupidity and lack of worth, with more supportive and positive reinforcement from fellow artists and customers in the craft show circuit. I took huge risks each time I quit my secure health care career a total of three times) to devote full time to Art. Each day presents new challenges to my sense of self-worth, which is so often tied to money. It IS OK to be both financially successful and happy in work and life. I made a box shrine to focus my intentions on happily making money.

Choose a small and sturdy box, Mine is 6" x 4" x2". Pick a topic on which you want to focus POSITIVE Energy in the coming weeks. Choose appropriate paper and symbols from the pockets in your Transformative Journal (p19-21). Using acrylic gel medium, start collaging from inside out. Select four objects of equal height for legs. I used Mahjong tiles. You may have to employ a stronger glue (*E6000*) for combining non-paper items.

(continued on next page)

• Find a phrase, a charm, or a symbol that expresses your intention and place it inside the shrine—or make a small version of the All-Purpose Icon (shrink the pattern size on your printer) and set it on a base inside your altar. As you discover additional charms, phrases, and symbolic images, add them. Place the shrine where you can see it in passing every day, where it will remind you to focus on your dreams. I used green to represent the color of US dollars. Money is a way to buy myself time and freedom, rather than Stuff.

• How is your relationship with your Self? What would you like to leave behind or change? How can you symbolize that? Make a shrine to your personal creativity, one with a box to enclose the things you want to be rid of with a New You outside. One box above another, like In My Grandmother's House, (below right), illustrates different levels of change. An early Grandma on top, a happy family photo in the middle, and a sadder and more abstract figure below, with a dead moth inside a watch case to represent the watch business that my great grandfather lost during the Depression.

• Create a doll who can hold a box of dreams, one standing in an enclosure representing the past, with a representative of you opening doors into the future. Look at the work of other artists, ancient and contemporary. *Pinterest* is perfect for this. How do others use symbolism and how can you adapt or be inspired by their overall approach? Ancient Egyptians and Chinese buried representations of all the people and objects that would be helpful in the next life in the tomb.

• Make a box that represents your own life with symbols of the things and people you need inside it. The Child You inside a box that becomes the body of the Current You, which is inside the body of the Future You.

• As the Celts incinerated the burdens of the past year, write what you would like to get rid of on paper and burn it in the fireplace. A Solstice is a good time of year to "Bless and Release" the past or a too-long-cherished obsession. We can become too attached to our own failings or remembered slights. Acknowledge they exist and move on. Send your resolutions up in smoke where they can be seen.

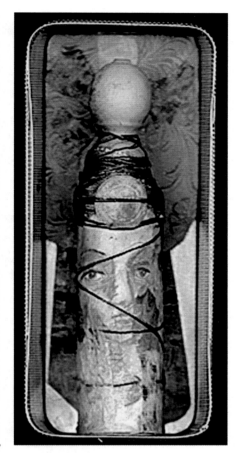

Spirit Grinder
2007 7″ Built inside a metal box.
I was feeling bound to the body.

In My Grandmother's House
1990's 14″ Levels, symbolic arti-facts and Xerox of photos

Amy Chester: Transforming the Self

"I came upon the art of doll making by accident. I happened to see a doll maker at an art show in September of 1997. She had many fanciful dolls in her booth, but there was one in particular that grabbed my attention, that spoke to my heart, and called to me so strongly that I was compelled to buy her and bring her home. I had never before been touched so deeply and attracted to a piece of art. To this day she hangs near my bed and is a comfort whenever I look upon her. Before then I had never seen dolls used as an artistic medium, and had never even thought of dolls in any other sense than as a child's toy. My eyes and my imagination were opened as I learned about the world of Dolls and all they can be.

"A couple of months prior to that day I had gone through a miscarriage with my first pregnancy. While I had spent the summer mourning my loss, I found I had become fascinated with art that illustrated humanity with all its beauty and varied colors. I had been searching for so many years that when I began to learn about dolls as an art form, I realized that I had found my medium, my true voice. I had found the means to create using all that I had learned, using all the materials and techniques that I loved, and creating an end result that would seem larger and more powerful than the sum of its parts.

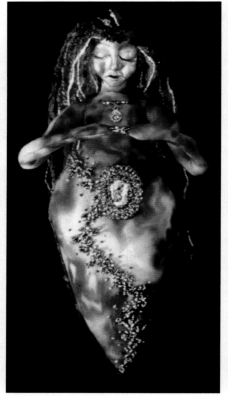

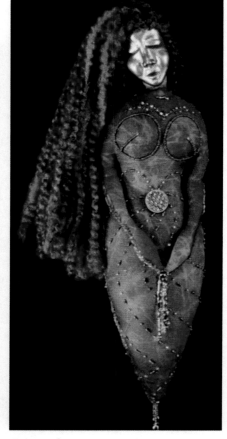

Azira

Amy Chester She sings among the birds and Dances with the wind. She flies ever onward, Journeying home.

Reverence

Amy Chester She lives with the earth and listens to the gentle song beating beneath the soil.she will remain.

Cassandra

Amy Chester Mistress of the deep, bringing energy from the ocean waters. Let her come and revitalize you.

I don't know if it was that particular time in my life that left me open to the art of dolls or if I'd have felt the very same in different circumstances. Looking back, I've thought that perhaps in healing I was driven to create something in place of what my body had chosen to give up. I realized that I had finally broken through my frustration and found a means to release the indescribable energy I had churning inside me.

"I create my dolls because it feeds and nourishes my spirit to give form to that which is inside me. I create intuitively with very little planning, attempting to tap into the stream of creativity I believe is a part of the human spirit. When I've attempted to design and make something with the purpose of selling and making money, I've found that others may be satisfied, but I am not. I feel that I've not been true to myself, and then the familiar nagging frustrations return. I have realized that only by pouring forth the energy and emotions I feel, by letting go and letting my inner self guide me, am I satisfied. I've found that when I am able to do this, people respond more powerfully and my dolls find their way home in someone else's heart."

Reverence

Amy Chester She listens to the gentle song beating beneath the soil. She will remain.

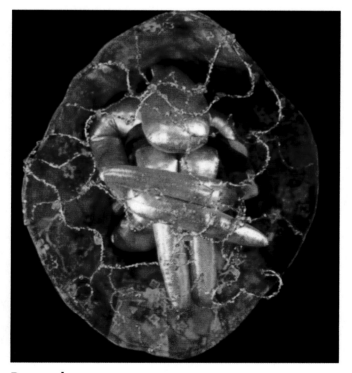

Renewal

Amy Chester

59

Transforming Relationships with Others

Old Schoolhouse
East Ryegate, Vermont

I grew up moving every year while my father completed his medical training through the VA. Art and my sewing projects kept me company. We inherit the ways of our parents. How else do youngsters know how to progress into parenthood themselves? They add as many improvements as they can, but my mother passed on her extreme insecurity and low self esteem but also exposed all of us to art and encouraged our efforts.

Dad's skill as a psychiatrist was not sufficient to keep me from marrying a man whose poor self image prompted him to be physically and mentally abusive to me and anyone vulnerable.

We lived the typical abusive format: isolation, both from other people and more positive kinds of feedback for me, in an old two-room schoolhouse in northern Vermont, where I let him create my Reality. We theoretically worked together as leather crafters. Even though I earned most of the family income, cooked, cleaned, gardened, toted the firewood, paid the bills, and kept our unit functioning, I lived in constant fear of saying, doing, or even suggesting the "wrong" thing/looking the "wrong" way. I had permanent bruises from being hit when I annoyed him, my left arm and leg sore from his blows in the car. I had been taught that the wife was supposed to accommodate to the husband's needs/wishes/desires and that marriage was "til death do you part." I was tempted to follow the family tradition of suicide as an escape.

Doll Making Saved my Life. That statement got your attention, didn't it? And it's true. I started the first edition of this book when I realized that if it hadn't been for doll making and Soft Sculpture in the Seventies and the warm and supportive people I met through the craft fair circuit, I might have plunged the black-handled butcher knife into my husband's fat stomach as he slept—or he would have succeeded in his attempt to shatter my spine and make me totally dependent on him that hot August night in our isolated Northeast Kingdom home.

Seeing Lenore Davis' work in Boston in the Sixties inspired me to evolve my doll making into soft sculpture. I realized that I could paint on muslin as I had on canvas. I encouraged my husband's interest in women even younger and more vulnerable than I was, including one with MS, which slowly, slowly earned me the space to start doing more on my own, including doing craft shows independently where I met a group of people who did NOT react to me as inept and generally awful, as I had been conditioned to believe. It took me five more years to work up the courage and timid sense of self-love to eventually leave him, having mailed my beloved journals and art work to safety, running away myself when he was away for the weekend, hiding with friends and gradually growing into who I am today—still growing. I talk about my own evolution hoping to give others courage and the revelatory gift of self-love with my example. I felt I had to have the two abortions to keep from being locked to him for life. Choice is important for All.

Even now, 33 years after leaving him, writing this, watching a movie featuring abuse, starts my stomach to roiling. People who say, "Oh why doesn't she just leave him?" don't understand the total interdependence of this wretched dynamic. For twelve years of marriage and the four years before, I, an intelligent woman, ignored all the evidence and BELIEVED that I was constantly in the wrong and unworthy of this talented man who just could not quite succeed because he had to deal with all the pressures of the world PLUS my constant stupidity and mistakes. That trap exists in many different guises, as I learned in subsequent job experiences. Several lifetimes later, I know that growth and change are a long and sometimes arduous process. No experience has been wasted along the way.

I have seen this syndrome in enough others to want to speak out, and I hope give courage to those who are suffering in this hell. We are blessed with the opportunity to take ourselves in hand as raw material and go on, constantly growing into who we will become, as long as we breathe.

Yukio Mishima

1980 5' Painted and quilted muslin on stretchers, bright red rayon guts, from my Yukio art series prior to leaving my husband.

Angry Woman Mask
1980 Painted muslin, satin, lame,
quilted over armature wire

Remembering
1989 Mixed media

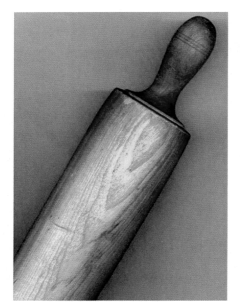

Great Uncle Billy's rolling pin once
for self-defense, now only for, pies

I knew I had to leave five years before I actually worked up the courage to do so. I mailed my most precious possessions, my journals, to a friend in Massachusetts. In my last year in that isolated school house, I worked on a series of paintings, collages, and finally a five-foot tall soft sculpture about the writer Yukio Mishima's ritual suicide. Expressing the blood, anger, and the inwardly-turned violence of Mishima's death helped to channel my rage until I could get to safety.

Working with angry images over and over allowed me to start feeling more comfortable experiencing and expressing my own rage. As I was growing up, my mother had periodic noisy emotional outbursts which were quieted by a shot or a pill from my psychiatrist father. Later I realized that she was experiencing the female-oppressing Fifties and post-partum depression, as well as inherited chemistry. It took a long time and many art works for me to stop associating anger with craziness, and to gradually move toward feeling justified in experiencing and expressing my own feelings. I'm still working on feeling compassion and love for my mother when I am with her, as opposed to living several thousand miles away.

Close to the time when I actually did leave the Schoolhouse, I got mad and yelled at my husband, as I stood in a doorway, protecting myself with a chair in front of me and with the rolling pin my Great Uncle Billy made for my grandmother. The dents from pounding that rolling pin into the door frame remain today as a souvenir of my emancipation.

In my online classes on Doll Making as a Transformative Process, the inherent inequity in male/female relationships continues to be a popular topic, echoed by the inequities in relationships where any participant seems to hold an imbalance in power: governments, religions, corporations, the status quo as opposed to the outsiders. I have made a lot of art work based on my own family drama, back to grandparents and through my own adult life, starting a series of mixed media/fabric wall hangings with my own stories in 2014.

Coming from a lineage of archivists, I see how family baggage is passed from generation to generation to generation with slight alterations. If we are mindful, there are improvements. In my mother's 90's, with her Depression-era difficulty in getting rid of possessions, I understand better how our possessions represent us and our desire to continue our presence through the years.

I practiced mothering on my four younger brothers, deciding that I wasn't up to the challenge of mindful child rearing. I saw the toll that postpartum depression took on my mother and the rest of the family. I never found a real partner. My art, my books, my students and my brothers are my progeny.

Initially I found it easier and less threatening to use art themes that were a generation removed. My mother and I have had some stormy times, and I continue to work through my relationship with her in art. I appreciate how difficult her own life has been and how much she has supported my artistic aspirations, so I keep my work about her relatively private and don't force her to confront what she could not help.

It can be difficult to separate the art from the subject of its story. The finished product is for its creator, but the work is Not the artist. Expressing ourselves in words and tangible form can help us to understand the forces that have shaped us, and to put them at enough of a distance to deal with them, instead of letting them overwhelm us and maim yet another generation. Learning and growing never end.

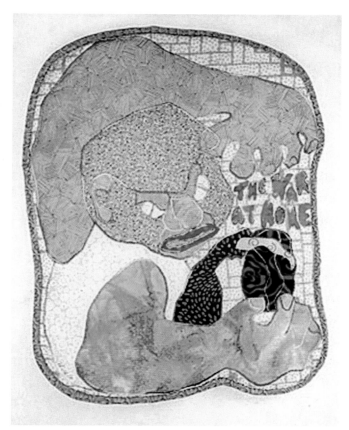

The War at Home
2003 18″ Fabric, quilted, made for an exhibit about war.

And Then She Left
2014 20″ Fabric/mixed media. About leaving my last relationship and working out my life history in art.

Working with Family History

I use containers and words to represent layers of meaning. I have frequently used images of my grandmother and her ancestors to address issues of how I got to be where and who I am now. It was less scary to use my grandmother, who was not around to comment, than my mother, who was more aware of my art production ten years ago, but is less so now. There is often a conflict between not wanting to hurt the people whose images and stories we use in our art work and needing to express what we must express as artists and as self-healing humans.

The Grandmother Box sets the family scene, with Xeroxed images of my Grandmother's wedding in 1918 and family homestead on the box, and herself as a young woman with an Eighteen Nineties shape on the top. This piece may be more descriptive than emotional, but by describing a relationship, event, or interaction you will find yourself discovering new relationships, new layers of meaning, and new personal symbolism.

The wedding photos on the outside of the Grandmother Box and the way I remember her telling the story was that she was very surprised and delighted that someone actually wanted to marry her. She struggled with an extremely poor self image as an ugly duckling, even though she looks lovely to me in pictures.

I constructed the box around a found picture frame. Now I would probably just cover an actual box, but I made stiffened sides (buckram under fabric) and added an armature wire frame. I still tend to sew, rather than glue, making the creation a meditative process. The embellishment evolved during the construction process—lace, beading, running stitch, buttons.

How and what will our own great granddaughters know about us, and how will we pass the information along? Will FaceBook postings and YouTube videos be enough to explain who we were and what was important to us? Is that important? Will people always want to know about their ancestors?

Grandmother Box
1990s 15" Soft sculpture, wire armature, Xerox copies of grandparents' wedding photos, lace, beads, lame.

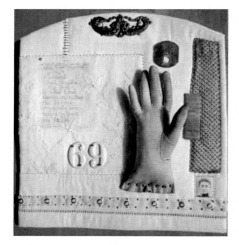

When I Married
2014 20" Fabric, stuffed kid glove, lock, ancestor photo on cotton, writing on fabric, plastic numbers for wedding date. I'm still using my history cathartically.

In My Grandmother's House: The form is the shape of a woman with my grandmother's face at the time of her high school graduation on top. As I said, she was overjoyed to marry her handsome third cousin, and the growing family, my grandmother holding my mother is shown on the middle level. Unfortunately the happy family group seems to have been more of a myth than a reality. I think my grandfather was more of a lost soul than a dependable family man during the Depression, spending long periods away from his family looking for work, more than with them. He eventually committed suicide when my mother was twelve. Grandmother and her four children had to return to live with her mother and Nepolianic father on the Leonard Homestead in Northern Vermont. The homestead and potato farming were the only things left after the Depression, but apparently my great grandfather tried to rule the small Northeast Kingdom town, along with his family.

The words I've embroidered around the house/home add to the ambiguity of the piece, the potential for the viewer to extrapolate to her/his own situation. "It wasn't what I expected." Much like life for each of us.

By working with the images and materials an evolution occurs in which we lavish time and attention on symbols of a person or situation that may have initially caused us discomfort in some way. The time and attention can lead to healing. Like the obsessive dots in Australian aboriginal painting, spending time with/in creating, rather than just going around in circles in our minds can lead to resolution.

The watch in this piece represents the inheritances of the past, as well as the fact that the family had owned a profitable watch company, though this fortune was lost during the Depression. The figure on the bottom level is an abstracted representation of my grandmother in the photograph, but it also represents me as an artist and an inheritor of my grandmother's emotional legacy with the added power to change that inheritance into something positive for my own life. How would your family look in 3D?

In My Grandmother's House
1990s 18" I built an armature of wire and heavy-duty interfacing to show the different levels of her life. Found watch casing with moth, for my great grandfather's lost business, the Leonard Watch Company

Kate Owen Leonard
2013 8" My great grandmother Now we can print scanned images directly onto fabric, instead of using Xerox on paper

Transforming Interpersonal Relationships, Moving Through and Beyond Anger, Getting Past Helplessness, Seeing More Clearly

Doll making can be used to work on relationships, to understand and come to terms with emotionally-charged relationships and emotionally-charged Life Passages, moving through and beyond anger, getting past helplessness into action and even forgiveness. Anger is not always a bad thing, although I was taught to be afraid of feeling and expressing anger. Losing control could be dangerous, but anger can also be a way to gather and focus energy to take action.

Anger, like what my husband used on me, was his way of keeping me subdued and doubting myself. I have had employers who have used the same tactic. There is a complicated web of violence and care taking, of abuse and worship that keep people bound in or returning to a relationship that hurts them men-

tally and physically. The man (usually) creates the family's or work place's entire reality. We must access our own power in order to break free, creating a very different image of ourselves from the one we probably learned as a child and that has been reinforced or recreated by our abuser. Justified anger is a powerful tool.

Making dolls and creating strong images gave me the courage to leave my abusive relationship. My mother's praising and supporting my art work, even though she didn't give me the role model of a strong woman, helped me to believe I deserved better than I was getting at home. I still need to remind myself I'm OK, even when I don't say yes to anything anyone wants. Set Boundaries!

Young Parents Shrine (Closed)

Young Parents' Shrine (Open)
2003 Cigar box, mementos and pictures from my young parents' courtship.

People have used repetitive story telling through the centuries as a symbolic way to understand what's happening to them and to create new and more appealing ways to explain the past and future.

I use the box form like a stage set upon which to play out stories. How do we learn to be adults and take our places in society except from our parents and grandparents? How do we learn to raise and care for our children except from our mothers and fathers? How do we learn to love and cherish ourselves and expect the same from others? Some of us must learn slowly and painfully from therapists and books, or on our own by experimenting with and adjusting what we do. By spending time working with the images and ideas, an evolution occurs in which we can lavish time and attention on symbols of a person or situation that initially made us uncomfortable.

You can see my experimentation with the connection between the two figures. Non-realistic heads, some found, takes away the necessity to be too lifelike in the dolls, although in collages, I've used copies of photos, sometimes drawing over the faces.

The stage is an old sewing machine drawer with spools glued on for legs. I had used plastic medicine containers (reminiscent of my mother's use of medication) on the Young Parents Shrine but the glue didn't hold on plastic. Now I might use Apoxie Sculpt, which is non-toxic and great for combining found objects.

Positive Mother Collage
2003 In which I realized how much my mother's support has meant to the development of my art.

Mother, What did you Want
2004 Soft Sculpture conjoined
figures in a Sewing machine drawer.

Mother, What Did You Want?
2003 10" Antique doll heads,
fabric bodies, conjoined arms.

These sculptures were inspired by a dream my mother described to me, where her feared grandfather on his Morgan horse was tall enough to reach into her second floor bedroom window at night and grab her. The Napoleonic tyrant grandfather, who had to take his daughter and her four children in to the family homestead, the last remnant of his fortune. I wondered if my mother was molested. Her dream story returned to me when I started this book in 2003.

I found Mary Wornov's *Wake for the Angels*, in a used book store, reminding me of the vocabulary of line/words/form I had been developing while living isolated in the Old Schoolhouse. I had abandoned that good avenue of exploration along with the bad when I left my abusive husband to live in small apartments and struggle to make money with soft sculpture at craft shows.

My art work was interrupted by home and garden tasks with my second long-term partner, but I started to draft a complicated pattern from my rough sketches. In confusion about reversing a difficult pattern, I ended with two mirror-image figures on horses. and used that opportunity to illustrate two sides of a story. The red painted figure, Inherited Nightmare, represents my great grandfather, gripping my child mother in a white dress. The figure on the right represents me, the artist, taking charge of fears, and using the power that my great grandfather demonstrated, but in more positive ways.

In the exercises with Relationships you'll see th at perception of size/power does matter. Use extremely simple shapes to create interactions and stories between two or more figures. Adding talk balloons, which can be phrases cut from magazines, adds another dimension. By using the same simple shapes over and over again and taking serial photos or scans, you can tell a story. If you are having difficulty with a particular person, try setting up a simple paper representation of your latest interaction using strips, squares, triangles of paper and cartoon faces. Put the simple paper dolls in varied positions next to each other to express your relationships. Make thought balloons in different colors for what was said and what you were thinking. Try to imagine a thought balloon for what the other person was thinking, too. Are the words very different from the thoughts? Practice changing scripts with the doll that represents you. Is there a new script that feels better once you move beyond feelings of anger or helplessness?

When you work to imagine what the other person was thinking, does it help you to understand better where they might be coming from? Now use your imagination to create a different ending between your figures. Is this a solution you could use in life?

To be more elaborate, create a box stage and make your figures with bases and jointed limbs. Act out your drama and create different endings—psychodrama in miniature. See Lani Gerity's work with puppets and therapy. You could have group members experiment with different roles and alternative solutions.

Be sure your "stage" is big enough for everyone to see, and that your group can be supportive, non-judgemental, and can handle whatever comes up. Are you an effective group facilitator?

Scream
1970s 14″ painted muslin and satin, part of a word series I did in the Seventies and sold at craft shows. Pick a word from your journey to illustrate.

Simple paper shapes, acting out a situation where one person has all the power.

Resolution and acceptance

(Pattens on page 75)

69

Davina Murry: Transforming Relationships

"You asked about experience with Healing Dolls. My story is about a doll that healed. He was the first ever cloth doll I made when I was a young wife, pregnant with my first child. I was eighteen years old and coming to terms with the fact that the gallant, handsome young man I married was an abusive emotional cripple The happy marriage I envisioned was not, try hard as I did to make it so. We lived in the country, about half an hour from town and about three and a half hours from my family. I was allowed no friends and not allowed out alone. I felt I was in prison, sad, lonely and betrayed. My heart was broken and I was miserable. What had I done to deserve this?

"I had always loved playing with dolls as a child. I couldn't go to bed unless I checked to see they were all right side up and tucked in their bed. I dreamed of having babies and and the happy family we would be, so my reality hit hard.

"I had an old sewing machine, and from pieces of fabric and used linen I made a flat-faced floppy clown doll. It reminded me of me, the painted smile but the 'floppy' soul. I made clothes that could be taken off and washed or changed. He was my inspiration. Something I had put energy into worked! Maybe it wasn't all me! He brought a smile to my face. I had found an activity that made me happy to fill my day.

"From then on I found strength to start to challenge myself to make decisions about the rest of my life. Did I really want my baby to grow up in a household of fear, to witness her father beating and berating her mother?

"I insisted we take counseling and to my surprise, he allowed it. He thought the counselor would 'sort me out.' Right in one way, it took me a while to grow the courage, but by the time my daughter was one year old, I had left, moved to town, and set up my own little nest. It was hard to do, and that clown doll was my inspiration.

"I have been married thirty years now to a kind and loving man and my thirty-three-year-old daughter has just had her first child. My clown doll is in New Zealand at my deceased mother's house.

When my step father dies I will go and reclaim my healing doll."

Davina Murry is a happy doll maker who lives in Queensland, Australia

Andrea Cooley

You see them like this
in the grocery store.

Women. Frozen.
Just trying
to get through the day.

Things are never
quite the same
after one eye explodes.

It happened to my aunt
that way.

Death. Divorce.

And through it all
she wore that lovely
flowered outfit

and smiled all the time
through the groceries
and laundry
and dinners.

Suddenly,
one eye exploded
and she saw all the wires
wrapping her up.

Except for that one hand.

One hand is always free.

We haven't seen her since.

Andrea Cooley was an occupational therapist and MFA Student in 2003.

not knowing what to do
in the days preceding the divorce

and finding it impossible
to manuever in tight corners
I decided to cut off my fingers and the top of my head

an act of self mutilation you might say,
you might be worried about my mental health
and how I was holding up
under the stress

I was worried too at first.

I felt compelled to find twigs and branches
for my fingers,
wild yarn for the top of my head

But nothing was right.

The color was wrong. The weight was wrong.

I worried I might lose all my insides
the minute my head flopped over.

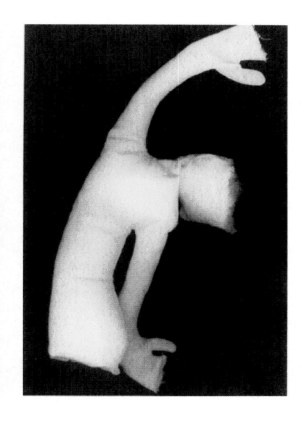

So I stitched my edges,
packed myself in tightly
and flopped around a little.
Let it all hang out you might say.

Nothing fell out.

I began to feel lighter.
Not like I had wings or anything,
but freer.

You might point out that I can't hold on to a single thing
with no fingers.
Can't keep a thought in my head.
They all float out the top.

That is true.

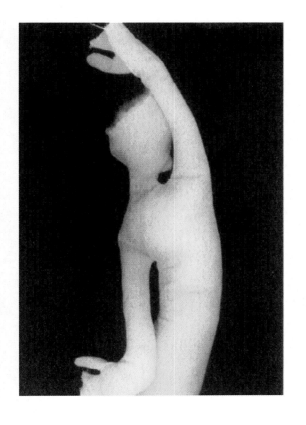

Stretching
inside this black box

and waiting.

Doll and poem by
Andrea Cooley

*In 2004, I didn't own a digital camera, but now we all
can easily take sequential photos of simple cloth or paper
dolls to tell stories or create group myths and reenactments
of family dramas.*

Playing with Size and Position to Express Relationships

Self-Portrait Paper Doll
2004 12" My many parts interact in this round paper doll. We have relationships with the different aspects of ourselves.

If the participants in a relationship have unequal levels of power, express that by exaggerating key body parts. One figure may be large, learning over a smaller figure or one may be all mouth and no ears. Some time after I finished the first edition of this book, I realized that I was making many of my dolls without mouths—my outdated concept of Relationships, in which the woman was all-nurturing, and the man (my training) dictated everything. If I ever engage in another committed relationship (beyond friendship) with a man, there will need to be a lot of negotiating. I see more couples creating individual living spaces.

Simple doll shapes can interact in photos or in person to tell stories. Use paper doll versions of these patterns, if you prefer. The Menacing Male has enlarged hands and arms to be even more over bearing. The rice stuffing in the yellow doll allows for lots of variation in poses. With Fiberfill stuffing, you can pin and ladder stitch the limbs into permanently expressive positions.
Use a copier or printer to enlarge the patterns. Collect photos in your Transformative Journal of strong expressions and simplify them for doll faces—or scan graphic novels. A computer search generates all kind of expressions.

Menacing Male
Male: scary face and teeth from car-patterned fabric, thin, droopy yellow rice doll. Pattern p.75, 77. Rice makes the doll easy to pose.

Doll making can be used for work on death and dying. Mourning for a person who was very close, like a parent or spouse, can take two years or more. As a part of this process, the negative as well as the positive feelings must be sorted out and acknowledged. Especially for a suicide or a person who died young or unexpectedly there are angry feelings that are not the whole feelings, but can be explored safely through doll making. Remember, it's OK to feel anger. It takes less energy to feel and express it than to keep it buried, where it can cause physical damage or make the sufferer more vulnerable to the diseases that are always present in our environment. Once the anger is acknowledged, a celebration of the person's life can be created with joy and sadness, as a way of moving on.

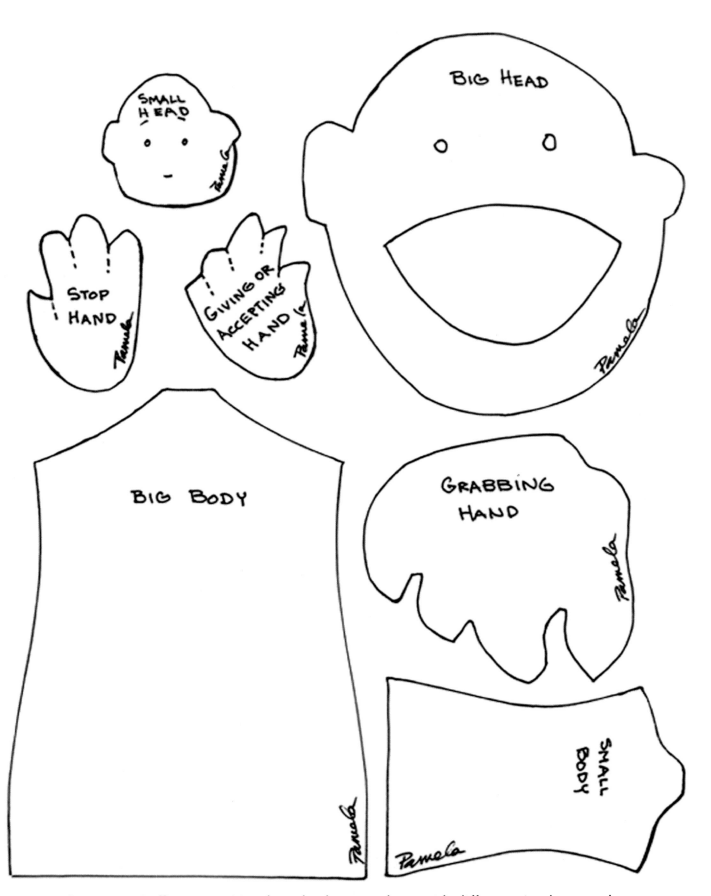

Size Paper Doll pattern: Use these body parts along with different sized rectangles, circles, and triangles to work out size/relationship dramas. Page 63

Gel medium or packing tape face transfer: Use a magazine face, since the ink sits up on a glossy background. Cover the front of the picture with a piece of clear packing tape or layers of acrylic gel medium, burnishing the picture into the tape or working the gel medium into the paper.

Put the paper with gel side down onto a high thread count light-colored fabric. Using a press cloth and no steam, iron the paper, gel, and cloth until all the water has evaporated. Put the cloth with the paper stuck to it or the packing tape with the image stuck to it into warm water for about ten minutes, until you can roll the paper fibers off the ink, which stays with the fabric or tape.

Use Mop and Glow floor wax applied with a paper towel to coat the image, making the colors shine. You can apply the tape face directly to cloth with clear gel medium or sew the face to the doll's head.

Ancestor Icon
With face printed on fabric and sewn to the body.

Magazine Face

Yellow Doll
Stuffing a simple doll shape loosely with rice creates a limp form that can be posed easily. Sad face on opposite side.

Rubbing Paper Fibers Off

Finished Face Sewn to Doll

Yellow Doll Pattern

Stuff loosely with rice
for easy posing

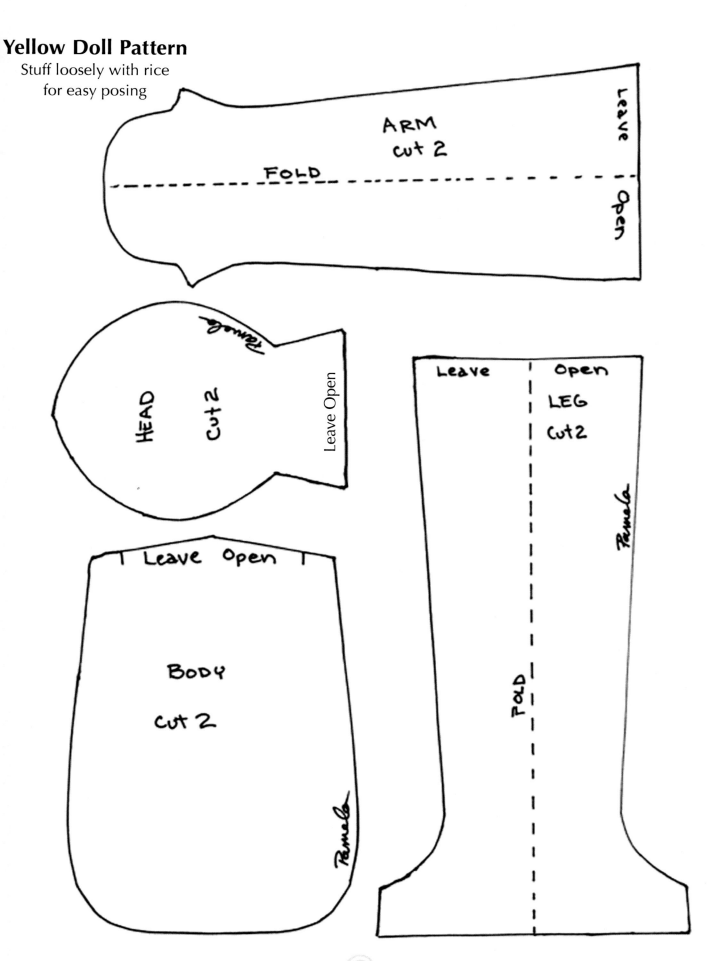

ARM
Cut 2

Leave Open

FOLD

HEAD
Cut 2
Pamela

Leave Open

Leave Open
LEG
Cut 2
Pamela

FOLD

Leave Open

BODY

Cut 2

Pamela

Blue Doll

In dealing with the death of a parent or special older person in your life, you may want to create a doll to commemorate the person at her/his best, as with the Ancestor Icon. Margi Hennen p. 84-85 tells a poignant story about living through her mother's deterioration from Alzheimer's disease, then realizing after she started her doll she was commemorating her loving memories of her family in happier times with *Emily Remembers*.

Sara Austin draws upon the physical and spiritual forms used in African art and writes, "Everything I do now comes from some story, usually a moment in my life that seems to be a turning point. I felt that since my mother's death the people I needed were always there, if only I'd let myself see them."

What are the spirits that guide and watch over you? What is your relationship with your Helping Spirits or family members who have pre-deceased you? Whenever I see a railroad train, I feel my father's presence, and now I'm dealing with my own aging.

You may want to do some research into Shamanism to explore historic relationships between humans and their spirit guides. It doesn't have to be concrete, more of an idea. Sometimes ancestors function as spirit guides.

Do you have an ancestor, real or an imagined, historical or book character that functions as a guiding spirit that you would like to celebrate in a doll? I can picture generations of women, opening out of each other or standing on the shoulders of the previous one—or suppressing the subsequent ones.

How would you express your relationship with your children symbolically ...how would they express theirs with you? Use these simple patterns or the All-Purpose Paper Doll and talk balloons to act out an interesting or challenging relationship in your own life.

I made the icon at left after a class with Barb Kobe when I was getting ready to leave my long-term partner in 2004-5.

Leaving Skip Icon
What does the missing left arm mean?

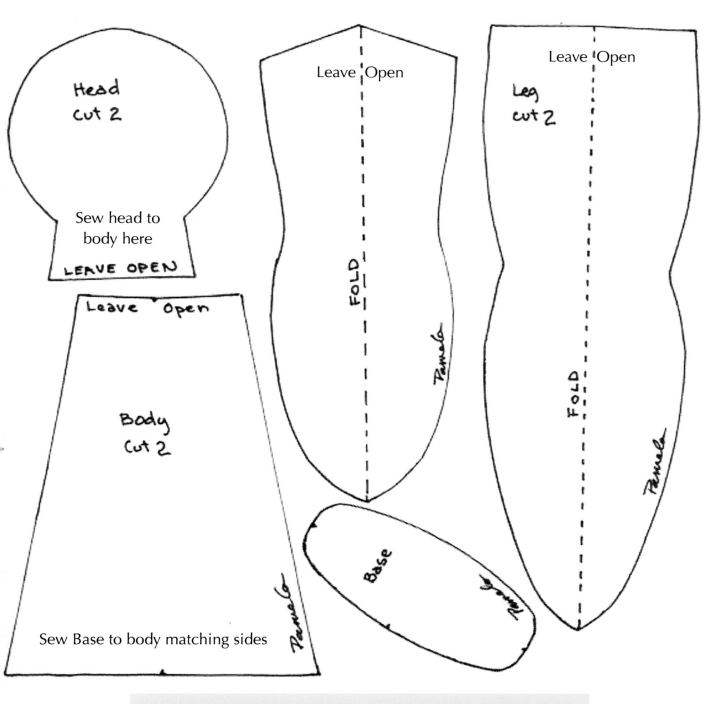

Head
cut 2

Sew head to
body here

LEAVE OPEN

Leave Open

Body
Cut 2

Sew Base to body matching sides

Leave Open

FOLD

Pamela

Base

Pamela

Leave Open

Leg
cut 2

FOLD

Pamela

Blue Doll Pattern

Feel free to enlarge or decrease the size of the patterns on a
copier or home printer. Adjust the size of the body parts for emphasis. Sew on the traced lines. tun and stuff. Sew head to body.
When attaching arms and legs, leave some looseness at joint to
make posing easier. Stuff with polyfill or fiberfil and tie joints
and waist. Pinch up a small nose and stitch to hold it in or add
any of the faces I've shown. You can use a ladder stitch to make
a pose permanent.

Christine Adams: Transforming Memories

Wedding June (Front)

Christine Adams

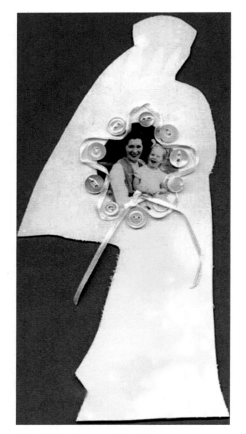

Wedding June (Back)

"When you first spoke of this effort, the spontaneous stories told in my art classes at the nursing home came to mind. It seems with residents that art is secondary to healing and humor.

"We've had a fine time working with doll making this year. Lots of stories emerged when we spoke of favorite foods. Even more tales were told when I invited the class participants to share family photos. Telling our stories has led to our understanding and knowing each other better. Laughter, sharing, and sometimes crying with each other have brought trust. We all look forward to being with each other regularly.

"WEDDING JUNE is a fabric book in the shape of a bride, using an enlargement of my Mom's wedding picture. Her name was actually June and she was wed in the month of June. The cover is Mom in her wedding dress. The pages are cut to match her silhouette, with photos attached with Wonder Under to give them body. The back of the book has a small embellished picture of me with my Mom. The pages are attached in accordion form, so it will stand upright.

"Nana Stump Doll is of my grandmother, Margaret Caroline Berger Landenburger Cummings. It has a simple cone base with collaged pictures and other fill all over the cone. Other than a picture of my grandfather, Otto Landenberger, all are of my Dad, Martin, and my Dad's mom, Margaret. I found that even residents on the dementia unit enjoyed making stump dolls. When photos were not available we used bits and pieces of cloth, lace, buttons, and other found objects. To give the cones stability, I stuffed them with newsprint."

We all enjoy having our experiences and history validated. It's a way of sharing between generations to celebrate the unique nature of the self. The tactile experience of assembling is even more involving. Celebrate your antecedents—they are part of you.

"Wedding Frances is a favorite, with several cloth dolls strung together on tape. These two facing dolls show Frances first as a young woman with the picture of her in a wheelchair superimposed. On the right is a picture of Frances now in her wheelchair over the shadowy yesteryear photo. We chose the quotes to layer on top of both dolls. Frances and I agree that the woman she is today was there but invisible when she was a young woman, and the woman she used to be is here, but barely visible in the woman she is today. She says that sometimes she looks in the mirror and catches a glimpse of her younger self."

Nana Stump Doll (Front)
Christine Adams

(Back)

Wedding Frances, Then and Now
Christine Adams

Christine Adams
Continues to use mixed media to create her own art and to work with students and elderly clients, for whom reminiscing can be very satisfying.

Parents and Children

Family relationships can be very complicated. Our families and how we are raised set the stage for who we will become, often creating mixed feelings in the process: separating versus embracing, how we relate to spouses and children, becoming parents to our parents, and creating enough of a distance from our parents to evolve into Our Selves and who we will spend our lives and energy becoming.

"Mother stories have to be told over and over," writes Kim Chernin in The Woman Who Gave Birth to her Mother. "Repetition is part of their nature. They have come into existence because, like a chinese box or a Russian doll, the innermost drawer of the meaning has been reached."

A parent is such a powerful figure in our development. We learn parenting from our parents, who needed no diploma in Best Practices in Child Rearing in order to reproduce. We may have generations of abuse, neglect, or simple ignorance to repair. As Transformative doll makers we can create our Good Mother and be mothers to each other. My own parents were so young when I was born, I should not blame them for their lack of perfection. I can only work to understand and empathize while striving to be more the way I want to be. I admit that I didn't have the courage to raise my own children. I foresee a life long task in giving birth to myself. Potentials for positive or negative influence are modified by circumstance and genetics. We are not doomed by our beginnings, and must take responsibility for the ultimate product that is our lives.

Self-portrait
2010 14" Wire hair, sequins, and wings.

Weddings of Grandparents and Parents
Fabric journal

When I was a member of Fiber Artists with Nerve group, I started a cloth journal Round Robin, sending stiffened muslin pages out to fifteen people on the topic of mothers. Unfortunately the project bogged down after the first round, too emotional to complete. Don't force a process for which you don't feel ready. BUT remember that there is usually an increase in discomfort just before a breakthrough. We dance with the material.

Several years later I did a successful Stories My Mother Told me Round Robin fabric journal project. The title was open enough to allow for both sweet and angry topics. Each participant could choose her own comfort level. From a distance of space and time, I can see how much my mother supported all of us in our art interests and still does. I work to treat her with compassion.

My first Christmas. My parents were 22, so young!

Angry fabric journal page when I was having boundary issues with my mother, fabric knives. (1998)

Margi Hennen: Mother/Daughter

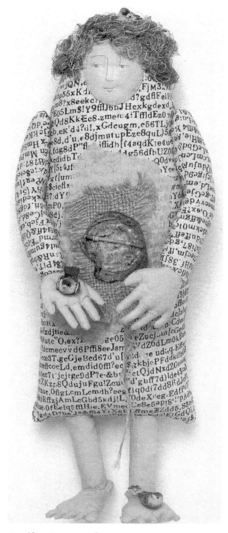

"*This doll started out with my desire to use some of the beautiful burgundy dogwood twigs harvested from my back yard. I then pulled out stuff I thought should go with their rich color, paper, and a flattened round of rusty metal. These things included a piece of white fabric with black typewritten letters which I had tea-dyed, a piece of brown burlap pulled at the edges, a bit of handmade paper.*

"*It was not until I put these all together that I realized that the whole piece was about my mother's Alzheimer's disease. The typed words on the fabric made no sense, the burlap was shredding, the paper torn, and the doll was in her bare feet, though she seemed to wear a dress—something my proper mother would never have done. I was initially really spooked by this. I remember wailing to my husband that I couldn't do this any more. However, I hung her on the wall where I could see her every day and ultimately her innate sweetness won out. I gave her a bird nestled in her hair and one on her foot. My mother loved birds. I named her from a song by Shirley Eikhart, EMILY REMEMBERS, about a friend who has Alzheimer's. 'She can't remember that I love her—I remember it for her.'*

"*I don't imagine that I need to tell you about all the conflicting emotions with which one is assailed when a parent succumbs to this disease, not the least of which is the totally selfish fear that it might happen to you. Somehow making this doll brought a measure of acceptance and a renewal of the respect and love I felt for the mother I knew before the disease changed her.*"

Emily Remembers
Margi Hennen

Margi Hennen and I met through doll making, which she pursues while her husband's job takes them all over the world. Her sense of humor and plays on words prevails. Many of Margi's pieces are subtly political. Perhaps Canadians are more polite than I. I've seen Margi dye her hair blue or purple and get silly with the rest of us. I commend her for being able to tackle potentially hugely emotional topics with kindness and good humor.

Diana

Margi Hennen: "On a warm day in the Ephesian forest, Diana can un-snap her breasts, slip them into her tit bag, and go on her way, offending no one... made in response to the arrest of a young female university student who reacted to a hot sum-mer day by removing her t-shirt in a public place."

Maria

Margi Hennen John Lennon lives on in Maria's heart.

Mother Warned Me
About Fishnet Stockings

Margi Hennen: "My mother was Presbyterian, and fishnet stockings were way too provocative for her. This doll's problems with fishnet stocking so far only involve a fish getting caught in them.

Margi's definition of a doll:

"Clever isn't enough - beautiful isn't enough. A doll is an inanimate be-ing that projects animation, a distillation of the views, opinions, person-ality of the maker. It may have two legs or three or none. It probably has a body of some sort (which could be a carrot). It may have arms - or not - or a tail, or wings. What it absolutely must have is life: a story which may be different for every viewer, or a mystery to all, but the being must speak, sing, SHRIEK her story."

Sara Austin: Mother, Daughter

Is It Safe?
Sara Austin

"I've had so many mothers. This thought has been in my mind for years, ever since my own mother died. I thought back to my best friend, Susie's mother, who was like a second mother to me when I was a little girl. And then I remembered this perfect moment of playing with our dolls, Susie and I, for the last time. It was perfect because we were together in our own world, sharing this stroller ride down the twilight street. It was perfect also because I knew we would never do this again. We were getting too old for this sort of thing. And I thought about the stages of my life, from birth, through childhood, into adulthood, and all the discoveries and adventures.

"Something was over, but something else was always beginning.

"Many motherly people surrounded me when my mother died. Then, when I no longer needed them they faded away. I thought about how we always have just what we need at the time we need it.

"I also thought a lot about African art, which is the art which had started me on the journey of doll mak-ing. It's the kind of art that is also life. There is no distinction between art and life. I strive now to live my life where all of my art has a function and all of my life is seen through the lens of art.

"Dolls came to me at a time in my life when I needed to make them. I was learning about mythology, read-ing the stories of Persephone and other myths, and images came into my head that I had to create. These were my first three-dimensional figures. There were faces in the front and back. I felt that they should be able to sit and stand like real people and that every surface should be covered, to say something from every point of view. It became a passion. I made quite a few dolls about my own past and issues I was dealing with.

"When my own mother was dying, doll making helped me survive the pain of this major loss. I made dolls about and for my mother and for myself. Some of them had her face, either drawn by me from photographs or I used transfer techniques to put images of her face directly on the fabric. In this way, I was able to put my feelings into the dolls. This work, combined with a lot of reading and soul searching, helped me to maintain a clearer perspective on death and the grieving process. I felt fortunate that I had this ability to make personal dolls. This was clearly dolls as therapy.

"To go back to the art of doll making, I am a strong believer in the creation of dolls as visual art, as psychological therapy, as toys, as teachers, as friends, and as guides. The idea of starting a doll making department in a college has occurred to me. The potential to learn about drawing, color, sculpture, psychology, cultural anthropology and history is there in these little stuffed figures. Dolls can be full of magic and power."

Only Give
Sara Austin

Summer Nights
1999 Sara Austin

Transformation of the Physical

More Crocheted Dolls

With Model Magic faces, expressing movement. Use symbolic colors and objects for healing intentions. Use a double stitch to make cylinders, stuffed with fiberfill

Our body's natural state is health. What factors cause or contribute to illness? What has led to the imbalance in the body that has opened our natural defenses to the bacteria and viruses, the environmental pollutants that assault us daily? What causes us to walk unsteadily so we fall and hurt ourselves? Why do we fail to exercise or eat healthy food? When stress gets to be too much, do we conveniently fall ill so we Must rest?

What purpose might the illness or injury be serving? What can be gained from the experience of Illness in addition to or instead of Health? I'm not saying that we are each responsible and to be blamed for each accident or illness. Bad things happen to good people BY CHANCE, and we don't always have the capacity to explain why. But who hasn't been totally stressed and then sustained the injury or come down with the flu that forces us to take the rest/time out that we haven't taken for ourselves?

Emotional injury and illness affect us physically as well as mentally just as physical incapacity affects us emotionally. I know from treating both kinds of patients that we can't separate the physical from the feeling aspects of our selves. Both healing and coming to terms with whatever wild card health has dealt us take energy and attention.

I feel very strongly from all my 25 years of educating patients that we must stop entrusting medical professionals with the TOTALITY of our health care and start taking responsibility for understanding how our bodies work and participating actively in keeping ourselves healthy, at least with exercise, stress management, and diet. Who should care more than we do?

When all else fails and we do succumb to an accident or unavoidable illness, a healing doll can help us focus energy to aid the healing process Take time to clarify your intention for healing body or spirit. When you make healing dolls for others, focus on what THEY desire as an outcome. Use their personal symbolism, or as Carolyn Myss says in *Sacred Contracts,* let your transmission of energy to them be in the form of asking the Universal Spirit to send your love and good wishes to the patient for the best possible outcome and the courage to learn and grow from whatever happens.

CHAKRA DOLL PATTERN

Two layers, trace,
sew, turn, stuff

8) Carolyn Myss adds an eighth Chakra above the head for archetypes

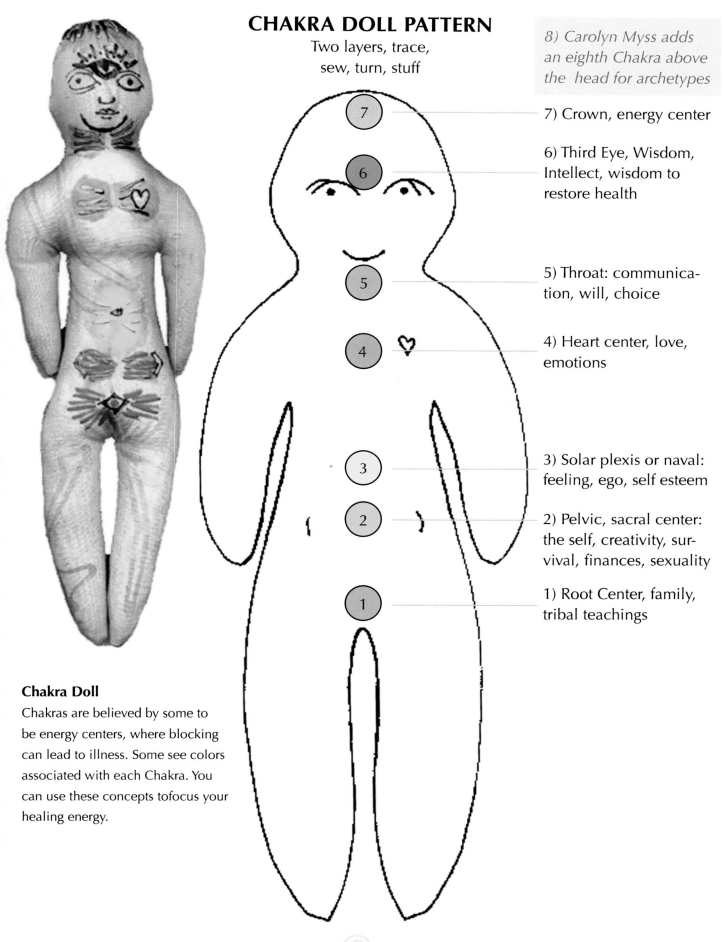

7) Crown, energy center

6) Third Eye, Wisdom, Intellect, wisdom to restore health

5) Throat: communica-tion, will, choice

4) Heart center, love, emotions

3) Solar plexis or naval: feeling, ego, self esteem

2) Pelvic, sacral center: the self, creativity, sur-vival, finances, sexuality

1) Root Center, family, tribal teachings

Chakra Doll

Chakras are believed by some to be energy centers, where blocking can lead to illness. Some see colors associated with each Chakra. You can use these concepts tofocus your healing energy.

Crocheted Dolls take on expressive poses. The Model Magic faces seem to form themselves, like molding marshmallow. Paint with acrylic.

Baby Goddess Pin

Karen Shelton She carries small dolls wherever she goes as luck charms and conversation starters. "What better way to remind us of the spark of the divine that we all have within us?"

I have discovered that I have work to do now in conjunction with the changes of aging. Becoming dependent on others for care is what I fear most, my decreasing eyesight and energy are frightening.

In 2004 medical studies showed that women with advanced metastatic breast cancer who attended support groups and had a vehicle for venting their feelings about the disease in addition to receiving conventional medical care survived twice as long as women who did not have the emotional outlet. Each case is different, but I know from my health care experience that there is an emotional component to every physical problem—mind and body are definitely connected.

We have only to look to the concept of the voodoo doll/power of suggestion to Bernie Siegel's story about a patient who heard doctors outside the room saying that death was imminent and promptly died. There are miracle cure stories on the other side of the coin. Biofeedback has become a viable treatment option for some pain sufferers. I participated in some of the early experiments with it when I was in college. Experiments have shown that imagery directly affects the autonomic nervous system which controls basic body functions and the immune system. When I wore my lab coat, patients subconsciously put greater credence in my healing powers and we could work together to heal them. Belief and involvement aid the effort. When the ill person feels that they have some control in the process, they are less likely to succumb to depression, and therefore can heal more easily. The inability to be aware of our true feelings can leave us at their mercy physically. Wizard of Oz is a prime example of patients needing to have faith in the cure to effect it.

POSTURE: Set your timer for two minutes and take the posture of depression—head down, shoulders slumped, spine curved. Feel the heaviness permeating your mind and body. Let your thoughts turn grey and hopeless. Feel the feelings so you will recognize how much your whole body becomes a part of negative thought. When your timer rings, do ten jumping jacks to clear your body, then stand upright, stretching to be as tall as possible. Raise your arms, look up, smile, breathe deeply and regularly, Imagine bright colors, pleasant images. Feel how your whole body changes.

Using the Chakra doll as a guide, mentally pass through the parts of your body, taking note, in a non-judgemental way, of where the tension is and let it float away. At the top of your head, be aware of whatever might enter by way of dreams.

In *Gate Theory* of pain management , only a certain amount of information can pass through our nerve receptors at one time—why a TENS unit works. I have seen total mental involvement in a project block out worries and pain, leaving space for the body to relax and heal itself.

A healing doll is a prayer made tangible, release healing endorphins into the blood stream or isolate and burn the "sick" part of an image. Our species' physical evolution has been slower than the evolution of our social and scientific systems and our ability to do damage to our planet and each other. The hippocampus and amygdala (storehouses of emotional memory) are the remnants of our animal emotional brain. The neocortex (thinking) brain is slower to take over under stress, leading to impassioned actions that we may later regret. Group actions like war or mob violence become frighteningly possible in the heat of the moment. Women had to evolve cooperation to care for the helpless young, and men still seem to be defending territory and goods. I see the women in my classes making dolls, changing their friends' and their own lives with small acts of courage, kindness and sharing. I envision ever-growing circles of loving kindness and Transformation for all—in time to save Home, I hope.

In Me, But Not Of Me
1990s 18" With a celluloid rattle that turns in its belly. We are NOT our illness.

VISUALIZATION: Visualize a doorway, opening into What? Where do you truly want to get to with this Transformative Healing Process? If you can picture it, you can facilitate it. If you don't know where you're going, how can you get there? This might be a good time to work with your Dream Journal and before you go to sleep at night, concentrate on relaxing your body from the bottom of your feet to the top of your head. Working in the present tense, write your dreams when you awake. I have been keeping a Dream Journal almost daily since 1969. It's interesting to watch my concerns as reflected.

Time, Time, Time
2015 12" Part of my aging series

Anger Management: The Dammit Doll

I discovered this doll and the poem when I was teaching in Mendocino in the spring of 2003 (my First Heroine's Journey). My thanks to Alice, who brought in the poem and her interpretation of this immediately-healing doll. Try making one yourself with legs long enough to grab onto and an amorphous body, not big enough to do damage, but enough to make a satisfying thump when hit against the edge of a table—not LIttle Brother, Please!

I don't think that enough women have yet learned to be able to express our anger without turning the emotion against ourselves. Maybe the younger generation. I know I still have difficulty. Maybe afraid that any display of strong emotion is too powerful, too Crazy. In order to feel empowered we have to KNOW that we are worth of love in spite of feeling anger, and we are not so powerful that we can cause actual damage with our anger. The others can protect themselves.

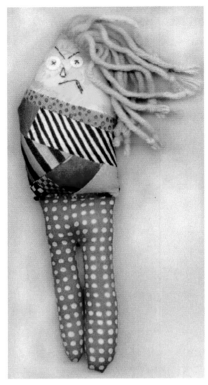

Dammit Doll

2004 12″ Follow the pattern on the next page. Regular use can be very healing.

Were You Ever Hit?
2012 10″ Mixed media Collage

Flat collages or dolls allow us to express the strong feelings that are safer outside of us than festering away inside. We don't have to share until ready.

When you think
You want to
Climb the Walls,
Or stand right up
And Shout
Here's a little Dammit Doll
You cannot do without
Just Grasp it firmly
By the legs
And find a place
To Slam it
Then as you wack
The stuffing out,
Yell
DAMMIT! DAMMIT! DAMMIT!

– Many thanks to Dayle and Alice

DAMMIT DOLL PATTERN

Cut two each of the legs and body. Sew the leg unit with right sides together, leaving the top open. Turn and stuff. Assemble and sew the two body pieces together along the sides, right sides together, leaving the top and bottom open. Put the top of the stuffed legs up inside the body. turn the body edges under and stitch the legs securely to the body. This joint could take a lot of stress. Stuff the body and insert the ends of the hair into the top of the head. turning edges under, and sew the hair securely in place.

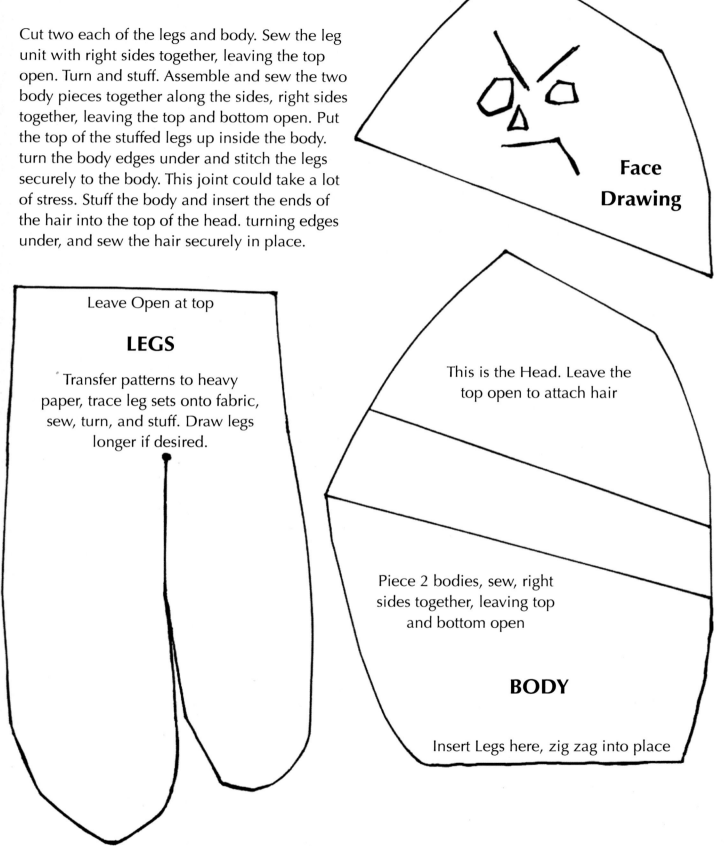

Face Drawing

LEGS

Leave Open at top

Transfer patterns to heavy paper, trace leg sets onto fabric, sew, turn, and stuff. Draw legs longer if desired.

This is the Head. Leave the top open to attach hair

Piece 2 bodies, sew, right sides together, leaving top and bottom open

BODY

Insert Legs here, zig zag into place

Kathie Briggs: Healing Dolls

"A few years ago i was working on a concept for a goddess doll It was late at night and I was still working in muslin. I thought, 'What would she look like with breasts?' I sewed the first one on then I saw my mother's profile in the doll. My mother died of breast cancer in 1987 and it was the eleventh anniversary of her funeral. My mother fought the breast cancer bravely, and I knew immediately I needed to make a doll that honors all the women who fight or have fought that battle. She has no face because she is Every Woman. Since then I have made other Courage dolls as remembrance or healing dolls.

"About six years ago, something about menopause unleashed a need to create. I live in beautiful northern Michigan where I teach cloth doll making through the local arts council."

Courage
Kathie Briggs For healing.

Guardian Angel (Closed)
Kathie Briggs

"This is an idea I played around with for a while. I made four angels. The first three dealt with all kinds of neat positive energy. The last one is different. Unconsciously I included images associated with people and pets who are deceased and much missed. They are all part of my personal guardian angel. You will see I included a miniature version of Courage.

Lisa's Doll

Kathie Briggs: "I made this doll for a friend who is pregnant and also facing serious surgery. I made it as an active prayer for her health and to comfort her. At the time I made the doll, the surgery was scheduled during her pregnancy, but her condition has improved enough that they are postponing the surgery until after the baby is born. The figure to one side is her daughter, the figure under her heart is the babe within."

Guardian Angel (Open)
Kathie Briggs

Cody Goodin: Healing Dolls

"Healing dolls are a physical manifestation of an intention for aiding someone or something. think of these dolls as a prayer in physical form. It is not the doll itself, but the energy it channels through the intent from which it was made.

"Use a simple body shape, decide on a theme, pick colors that will complement your theme. The is the color symbolism I use:

GREEN: General healing, promotes growth. Not a good color for those suffering from cancer.
BLUE: Used to bring a sense of calm and peace. Good color to use for any healing of skin, bones, and connective tissues
RED: Purifying color to cleanse the system of negative energies. Promotes courage and is good for healing sexual dysfunction.
ORANGE: Any ailment pertaining to the groin or sexual organs.
YELLOW: Use for mental disorders
PURPLE: Brings divine energy into play, detoxifying the body and emotions.
PINK: Heals emotional wounds or broken hearts.
GOLD: Attracts male and angelic energies.
SILVER: Associated with the moon, intuition, and female energy.

"The color of the thread you use symbolically serves to bind the energy together—white for purity and light, black to ward off negative energy, red to attract the energy of courage, and green for the most intense healing needs."

Ghost
Cody Goodin

Reborn
Cody Goodin A commercial baby doll transformed by paint and re-purpose

96

An internet search on healing and color reveals lots of further associations, including the colors of foods that could be used for healing. My feeling is that much of what we associate with magic/healing depends on personal choices and then the energy with which we and our healing client imbue them.

Cody's Color Associations:

Green: Balance, harmony, health, removing toxins. For curing skin disorders
Blue: Peace, calmness, cooling, soothing, sleep. For curing fever.
Red: energy, stamina, movement. For curing colds and anemia.
Orange: good digestion, joy, happiness, and a healthy sex drive. For curing allergies and asthma.
Yellow: Intellect, high spirits, good humor. For curing skin problems and indigestion
Purple: creativity, spirituality, inner wisdom. For curing diabetes

Greenman
Cody Goodin

Astrological signs are associated with colors and the body parts most likely to be affected. The Chakras have colors associated with them. Use what resonates with YOU and your client. Some use fairy tales as universal Jungian myths.

Carolyn Myss, an intuitive healer, uses character archetypes, such as the Warrior and a lot from Buddhist thought to help her clients perhaps step back from the immediacy of their personal stories to see their own lives more clearly.

"Herbs inside the doll as well as the color of the stuffing can be important. Be sure that the person being healed is not allergic to the herbs."
— Cody Goodin

Shaman
Cody Goodin

Shaman 2
Cody Goodin

Cody Goodin on Spiritual Transformation:

"I happened into making cloth dolls quite by accident. A friend of mine wanted something to use in her practice as a clinical counselor during her therapy sessions. She employed inner-child therapy as an important part of her work.

"Traditionally, teddy bears are used as a representation of the inner child. For my friend's birthday, I made her an inner child portrait doll out of cloth. Little Lizzy was born again. My friend just loved her and began ordering one for each of her clients.

" I have always been fascinated by human rituals. In doing research and reading on the history of dolls, I discovered that many cultures used dolls as ritual tools for everything from healing to keeping bad spirits away. This experience inspired me so much, I began creating dolls that could be used as talismans and healing tools.

"My work has been going through many levels of change over the years. I am finding myself gravitating toward less literal images and more symbolic figures. Most of this transformation is occurring on paper. It takes forever to get my ideas into actual three-dimensional form.

"I have also been doing a lot of inner exploration of my place in the universe at large. Where do I fit in and how can I tap into all of that divine knowledge so many seekers talk about? I have discovered, much to my disbelief, that everything can be found in silence.

"Even more profound than that is if you really want to see the truth in your art, heart, or soul, look into the spaces that exist between lines, the space between each second. In that place, or lack of, you will find infinity, all possibility, truth, and understanding.

"I came to this astonishing discovery when I began to look at sketches I had made for some new projects and wondered it there was more to art, to life. Then it hit me that in the spaces between lay the answers."

Life Passages and Transformation
Aging, Relationships, Hot Flash Women

My visual art and my writing flow directly from my life experiences. In the more than ten years since I wrote the physical version of Doll Making as a Transformative Process, Age has been making its inevitable creep into my life. I created the first Hot Flash doll way before I felt any of the symptoms myself. From the beginning I was determined to celebrate, instead of mourn.

After I had, for the third time, to go back to making my living in health care, I published *Hot Flash: A Celebration*, and started a series of 100 portraits of ordinary women, who are each remarkable in their own way. I'm up to 96, and having a project helped me through my last three years of working a regular job.

One of my projects in retirement from health care is to revisit scenes from my and my family's past in the form of small wall pieces. Everything I make now must be small, in order to be able to find space to store it.

Painting my own self portrait could be a way to stare at and become comfortable with the inevitable changes. This could be an effective group activity, along with the discussion. Our culture does not revere age/experience. What can we find about ourselves to celebrate? I don't get as bent out of shape as often as I used to—is that acceptance or resignation?

Hot Flash
2003 14" For Pamela Armas, with as much flash as I could put together. If a life passage is uncomfortable, why not celebrate, instead of mourn? I'm finding this more challenging as I age and lose abilities.

Man/Woman/Relationships
Woman more comfortable than man. I've decided to live alone.

A fabric journal project about my life and ancestors...another way.

Barb Kobe: Transformative Healing Dolls

Barb Kobe with Endangered Feelings Animals and Fulls

I met Barb more than ten years ago through the internet and our shared interest in healing dolls. She has developed classes in person and online to further the participants' process of doll making. She has created a game board sequence to help her students move through the process and is coming out with an eBook, The Transformative Art of Healing Dolls in 2015.

"Dolls and art have always been in my life. My grandmother was a seamstress, my mother did a variety of needle arts, and my father was always making things out of wood. I loved art—I often painted murals for school plays, musical productions, and dances. After one year in college (focusing on art) I entered the work world and spent over twenty years in the fields of engineering drafting, graphic arts, advertising, and print and multi-media production. The closest thing I did to creating dolls was making my own clothes.

"My career as a professional graphic artist shifted focus with the birth of my children in the early Eighties. I spent my time creating art with my son and daughter and encouraging them to express themselves, at the same time time never owning my creative life, nor speaking the words, 'i am an artist.'

"My journey of creative recovery began when I exposed myself to people who saw my creative potential and encouraged me to take creative risks. In small steps at first, I was beginning to give myself permission to create.

"In 1989 I built a set of characters to teach my children about emotional communication. As I made each of these soft sculptures I noticed that I would work through my feelings: anger issues when making Angerilla, grief with Crynoceros. I realized that making art changed my emotional state. I noticed that I could transfer a feeling from inside to outside of me and dialogue with it. Using the characters with others would bring about long conversations about feelings. I witnessed that many people stuffed their feelings and had never learned to talk about them. This was the beginning of my realization that art could be used as an instrument for change and growth. These characters were my first healing dolls."

"My current focus on doll making began with my discovery of Elinor Peace Bailey's MOTHER PLAYS WITH DOLLS. Elinor's book filled up my creative void caused by producing set after set of my feeling characters. I knew my characters were making a difference in children's lives, but they were draining me of vital energy. I wrote a letter to Elinor, grateful for her book and inspiration. She called me several days later and when I asked her what I should do about my exhaustion with making the puppets, she replied, 'If you're tired of doing them, stop. Something else will move in.' Not long after I witnessed my first art doll show, met the artist, and gave myself permission to try this new art form.

"The next mentor came in the form of Clarissa Pinkola Estes' book, Women Who Run With The Wolves. Each story, along with Estes' wisdom, fed my creative spirit and inspired more dolls. The Doll in her Pocket: Vasalisa the Wise, about infusing women with the Wild Woman's primary instinctual power, Intuition, and deepened my work and my relationship with myself.

"Estes says, 'Dolls are one of the symbolic treasures of the instinctual nature. For centuries humans have felt that dolls emanate both a holiness and mana - an awesome and compelling prescience which acts upon persons, changing them spiritually. Dolls are believed to be infused with life by their makers. They are used as markers of authority and talismans to reminding one of her own power.'

"The next step on my path was infused with creative energy. I was making two to three dolls a week, along with making the small sets of feeling characters—Numbful and The Fulls. I decided that my interest in Jungian psychology from reading this book was a deeper interest in psychology in general and art therapy specifically. I began taking college classes locally and paying for them by making sets of FULLS.

"Doll making was becoming the medicine my soul needed to mend; the thought of taking it out of my life was inconceivable. Making my dolls gave me a home, a path, a purpose."

Mother Earth Releases
Barb Kobe Death and letting go.

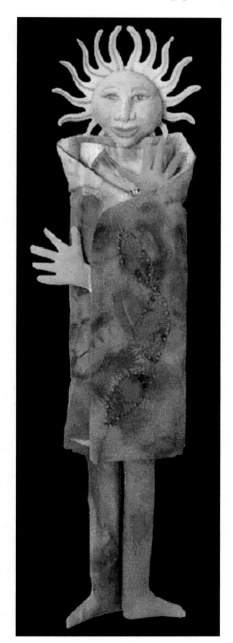

Dawn of a New Day
Barb Kobe

101

Digesting my Life

Barb Kobe

Saint

2003 Barb Kobe

"I knew that as I was creating my dolls, I was healing. I graduated with a BA in psychology in 1999 at the age of 50. As I created and taught the Dollmaking Circle my interest deepened even further into the subject of psychoneuroimmunology—the study of body-mind healing using images, specifically visualization.

"I tested out my theory by making a doll about healing an imbalance in my digestive tract. I cut branches from a curly willow and positioned them into an interesting body shape. I wrapped the shape with batting and then a deep purple fabric. After doing research on the organs of the digestive system, I appliqued the shape in the proper positions on the torso, with orange beads following the meridians (energy pathways). On the back, a symbol for the spine where all the nerves in the body connect. I made a Model Magic face with a veil over it, symbolizing going within, multi-colored hair representing connection with the mind. My intuitive voice kept telling me to wrap a yellow snake around her. Days later I read in Jeanne Acterberg's book, IMAGERY IN HEALING, that a yellow snake represents women's healing power, which supported my theory.

SAINT: I had been reading about feminist psychology and women's spirituality, and was raised in the Catholic Church. My Healing Dolls have an intention to heighten my consciousness about what I believe and change some aspect of my life—physical, mental, emotional and/or spiritual. I started this design remembering the images on the walls and the alter of my childhood church. Once the design begins in my head, it leads the way to my completion of the doll. As I continued my studies and worked on the doll, I started to connect with the messages the Church was giving to women—and Me—in the Fifties and Sixties: that I am unworthy of love, that I must take care of others first, and that I should always be a Good Girl, saintly. The dolls hands come together over her heart (self-love) and she is looking inward for self-reflection. The three rectangles at the bottom have little dolls resting inside: pieces of herself, having come home from being spent taking care of others. I used green to represent the heart chakra, red for women's sensuality, and purple for spirit."

102

WINTER SOLSTICE: "A woman I know commissioned a doll for a dear friend who was struggling with ovarian cancer. As the doll was to represent New Beginnings, I made Winter Solstice...a time to acknowledge that there is love, hope, and healing in the world as long as you make the time for it. There is magic to this sacred time...take time and believe."

Symbols: Halo is communication with self, Holly is blessing for the new year, Pine tree represents prosperity, magic, and growth. The talisman of prosperity anchors the blessing silver spirals of moon energy and healing energy. She holds small sticks symbolizing connection with Mother Earth, symbols on her abdomen of the uterus and ovaries, reflecting light, inviting focus and prayer."

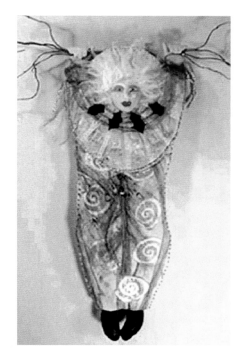

Winter Solstice
Barb Kobe

Barb Kobe's Ten Questions for creating a Healing Doll:

Each recipient of a healing doll must give the maker permission to proceed. I then ask the Ten Questions:

What colors are you drawn to and wear often?
What will this doll represent?
What elements describe you?
What symbols do you like and collect?
What part or parts of your body need healing?
What animal may have a special presence in your life?
When do you feel the most powerful?
When do you feel the least powerful?
What does your heart yearn for?
What is your favorite fairy tale, its meaning for you, its place in your life?"

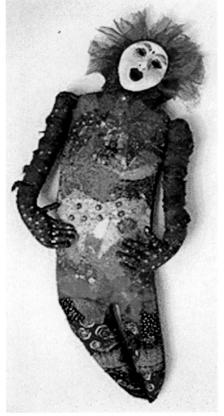

Chakra Doll
Barb Kobe Similar color choices to mine, in Barb's doll making style.

Spiritual Transformation

I see from my ten-year perspective that spiritual and physical transformation are inextricably intertwined. The mind and body are connected. Keeping both healthy will be our goal, and discovering the points in our past or current lives where the dis-ease enters, so we can do as much as we can to heal ourselves, and to help others heal.

It is a wonderful thing to be driven by passions! Too many in our culture are driven by advertising and the manufactured desire for new possessions—as soon as the energy crisis, the financial crises seems to be righting a bit, our lust for oversized cars is pumped up again. What is lacking in the lives that can be convinced that this is a good thing? The slump that comes in retirement with the loss of a well-structured, hierarchical environment in which to go to work. I am sorry for those whose purchasing is their only creative outlet. We are using up way more than our share of the world's resources on more and more Stuff that is less and less satisfying. Storage units are springing up all over. What happens as fewer conglomerates own more and more of the resources, with fewer people needed to manufacture the Stuff? This state has progressed even further in the last ten years. Will the world end with one last Rich Guy, sitting on a pile of consumer goods in the middle of a wasted, pollution-choked earth?

I lost interest in organized religion in grade school, when I began to see its inconsistencies. I have used "New Age" as a derogatory adjective in the past. As I've gained more knowledge, worked with people at the end of their lives, experienced 9/11 while on the way to the Seattle airport, read and studied more, I do see evidence in humans for a core need to make sense of our existence, our time in this particular plain of consciousness, and to connect with each other somehow, feel that our time has been spent with some beneficial effect. Nature drives us to procreate as the biological justification for existence, but is that All? We live so much longer than our ancestors. We don't all have children, and the planet is already choking from overpopulation. What legacy do we leave?

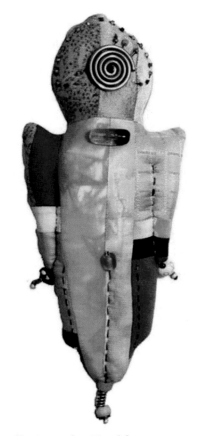

Studio Icon for David
2002 8″ Free-form piecing in his usual colors.

Studio Guardian for David
2015 10″ Body is a rusty metal box, doll arms, feathers, turkey bone, fabrics. So satisfying to meet the demands of attaching disparate materials to create a coherent whole.

The positive thing I see in the work I've done with doll making is the small circles of mostly women, beyond the distractions of the child-bearing and raising years, having time to explore our own ideas and creativity, work with our hands. I see the skills females had to develop prehistorically of cooperation and sharing ways of doing and information that we needed then in order to gather food and develop agriculture, that we need now in order to survive as a species.

The sharing that occurs in doll making circles is a kind of learning and wisdom: "I've been where you are now and this is what I did." It is nurturing, as we choose who our restorative mothers and daughters will be. The act of doing hand work now replaces some of the necessary tedious maintenance tasks of old and is also respite from the constant electronic stimulation and movement of today's world. The meditative quality of stitching gives us the space to be peaceful with one another and our selves.

When I participated in a group quilt project to raise money to fight an unwise cement plant expansion, I wrote, "Like most women of my age, I learned sewing from my mother and my grandmother. I see great hope in the phenomenon of women/people gathering together to sew, share wisdom, and work for a better environment for ourselves, our neighbors, and our grandchildren. Like the Slow Food Movement, perhaps this valuing of the small wonders of life will spread to the rest of the planet and reverse some of today's frightening trends toward bigger consumption and less regard for consequences."

In the print version of this book, I separated Cody Goodwin's contributions (p 88-89) into physical and spiritual transformation. As I write ten years later, I see much more intertwined connections between bodies and minds, people and the environment.

Some topics are worth revisiting again and again, each exploration leads to new ways of working with the raw material, as you can see by the differences in these icons for the same person.

I've arranged the chapters from inside, spreading out more and more into the world, but our environments, both in the family and in the world at large affect our spiritual and mental health and require our awareness and transformation as well.

Fulfillment

2000 14" I made this one for my brother 15 years ago, when he was trying to figure out what to do next professionally. We both had very demanding and highly-paid jobs, then switched to become self-employed and satisfied, having more time to make art.

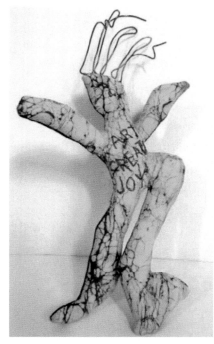

Studio Icon For My Brother
2015

Back Around to Transforming Our Lives Aging and Change

I am finding aging difficult. I always looked young for my age—until 65, when my thin skin started to collapse, my hair fell out, my belly started to become a separate entity from my Self and I didn't have the discipline to get rid of it, and I felt my energy dissipating. There is AL-WAYS Something to work on Transformatively. I have been aging since birth, but haven't been forced to confront the effects til now. I'm not adjusted to the Actual OLD AGE Aspect of my life, and different facets of it bite me at different times. I just gave up my bike, and am designing a painting about what we give up with aging, while I hold onto as much as possible as long as possible and search for new aspects to celebrate. I am circling my own eventual death with continued pieces about me and my mother and mixed media work on my family history, helping to light the way for those who follow.

Acrylic Painting

2008 8″ Words for me to live by. I have a history of boundary issues.

Symbols are shorthand ways of representing larger concepts, which you can research on the iInternet, but by working with Transformative ideas, you are developing your own personal symbolism, too. The symbol and the art work are ways of focusing your concentration on understanding and achieving your desired outcomes. This may be a way of mobilizing your body's physical and emotional resources to fight disease, allow the medical treatment to work as effectively as possible, or come to terms with challenging issues. There are times when the outcome is not perfect health or perpetual youth. The process of making the doll and meditating on the process can be used to come to terms with the reality of What Is, as opposed to what we want.

We may not be able to foresee a specific outcome that will be the Best. In my work with Palliative/end of life care, I was taught to LISTEN to the object of my care and what THEY want. In our culture illness, sadness, and death are often hidden, and we may find it difficult to talk about or even see this side of life. Making a healing doll for another person may help us come to terms with our own feelings about impairment and death.

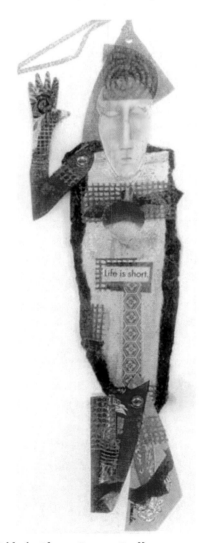

Life is Short Paper Doll

1999 I must keep reminding myself.

Accepting Who We Are

During body work I had an image of death as merely a dissolving back into everything else. Not a frightening process at all.

In my health care job I've heard many nursing home residents wishing for death, and it is sometimes difficult to stop reassuring them and simply listen. Dying people may accept the idea of death more readily than their friends and family can accept the idea of losing them. Be willing to listen and accept, to release the dying loved one. It may seem strange to pair the changes of menopause with illness, aging, and death, but any major life change that forces us to rethink the mental image we have formed of ourselves cries out for acknowledgement, and perhaps change. Maybe we need to find the strength to be our true selves in spite of what the world thinks about us at each moment of our lives.

We are the women striding across the boundaries of the Twentieth and Twenty-first Centuries. We are not just trying to genteelly conceal our sweat, but we are dressing in reds and purples and celebrating what we can't change. That is a big part of Transformative Art, even if women Still only make a percentage of the salaries that men do, bringing our changes out of the closet is the first step to becoming the fullness of who we can be.

Speaking of OUT OF THE CLOSET, parts of our society are beginning to accept the entire range of sexual orientation, family origin, and physical/mental skill sets.

All the individual struggles to accept different racial/cultural origins, different abilities in all areas could lend themselves to using dolls and art for Transformation. There may be learned or inherited boundaries to others' acceptance of us. There are times and places where being who we are could be dangerous. Can we nurture our own self love safely? Those who attack differences are doing so out of fear or learned behavior that could be unlearned.. Differently Abled

Tracy and Allison Stilwell's use of the hot flash doll concept. Safer to express Angry and Aggressive feelings in dolls.

Love Thyself
2010 7" Muslin, marker, embroidery. It's important to keep reminding ourselves about self love.

Transforming the World as We are Affected by Events

Angels

Each year I design a new angel to give to give to friends and family to celebrate the Winter Solstice and new beginnings.

Boxman (The Man) 1

2001 I was on my way to the airport in Seattle when the first plane hit the World Trade Center. I don't remember another time when the US seemed so vulnerable

"We shall require a substantially new manner of thinking if mankind is to survive," said Albert Einstein on the occasion of the atomic bomb first being used. I was born two years after that fateful moment, and the Doomsday Clock keeps ticking us closer to possible annihilation.

The human brain is wired for reproduction, empathy, and the improvement of the general lot of all. Just as our ancestor women had to work together to insure the safety of the children, the food sources, learning and passing on the information necessary for survival. The males went to war and killed things, more expendable once they had planted their seed, but needed to protect the women and the growing children. Evolution hasn't yet had time to unlearn some of the necessary reactions that insured the survival of the tribe in ancient times, like aggression, war, hating any form of "other" outside the immediate group. Using up current resources without regard to future generations. Each moment is crucial in determining which way the balance will tip.

I remember nightmares when I was perhaps four during the Korean war, vivid dreams of fleeing a burning city. In grade school I watched the McCarthy trials on TV and hid under my desk during nuclear war drills. I now live on a significant earthquake fault, under degrading skies and changing climate.

We may feel powerless as individuals to understand or change world events, but I believe the Transformative power of doll making can help there, too. As we have seen, we can change body chemistry by focusing positive energy. Cancer victims, working in support groups, can change the course of their illness. Therapists are using puppets and drawings to change the course of mental illness, performers and other small groups are changing their communities' appreciation and awareness of local political issues. Who knows? Perhaps doll making can Transform the world, circle by circle. Or at least help us to understand what is going on and our place in world events.

More than ten years after my first version of this book, I see Transformative art on more of a continuum from the personal to the Universal. I also see more clearly the value of working the same ideas over and over in different ways to increase clarity.

Visitors to my studio ask, "How do you develop your themes?" I see it as a dance between materials, symbols, words, the techniques that enjoy, like obsessive stitching, the events that impact my life, the challenging of combining different materials with found objects, solving problems in different ways.

I return again and again to themes, materials, techniques from my past.

Every living thing is both
intertwined
and totally alone.
When the planes hit the
World Trade Center
Life as we had known it
changed forever.
I thought of all the souls
trapped
in twisted steel...
When I was finally able to get
home. I completed this
figure, which I had started in
August, before the world
changed.

I have seen that toward the
end of life humans frequently
assume the posture with
which we entered life.

Everything is Connected,
Good and Evil...all ends of
every spectrum.
We do have the power to
choose and to change.

Pamela, October 2001

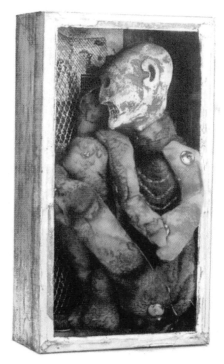

Boxman 1
2001 8″ Do you see a pattern of boxes unfolding? Tin box, collaged inside with photos of 9/11. Claustrophobic in his box/the falling sky scraper/the grave.

Boxman 2
2001 12″ When a theme is especially emotionally-charged, I find it helpful to revisit it again and again until I've worked through it. Two boxes this time with paper clay face, fabric legs, collage and words inside the box.

Eeo Stubblefield: Transforming the World

On Making Dolls in Eeo Stubblefield's performance piece *These Are Our Deaths* with permission from Mermer Blakeslee, photos by Violet Snow:

I performed in the provocative two-day piece, *These Are Our Deaths* out of both faith and frustration. Faith in the potent imagination of performance artist Eeo Stubblefield and frustration at American apathy toward our government's ruthless, calculated disregard for human life (specifically in Iraq).

I knew Stubblefield was going to use, in the performance, photographs of dead Iraqui civilians (mostly children) that she had downloaded from the internet, as well as those of grieving parents and grandparents, and newborn babies horrifically deformed from the effects of depleted uranium used in our bombs in 1991 (and still used in 2004). I was skeptical since I'm ambivalent about the graphic literalism of photography, especially in war, where it often desensitizes us to the horror, deadening our hearts to the very compassion it means to awaken.

What I didn't know or expect was the power of the dolls. Let me eplain. On the second day of Stubblefield's piece. We, the 15 performers dressed in black shrouds and veils, walked thee miles along the side of the road, gathering grasses and flowers to make our dolls--16 apiece--dolls dressed in white cloth on which the images of the dead had been screened in color. Carrying black bundles with twine, scissors, and the meticulously prepared dolls' clothing, we spent the day in a rhythm of gathering, sitting and making, walking, gathering, sitting and making, walking.

Eeo Stubblefield making a grass doll for a political action against the war in Iraq in 2003.

The dolls looked--with their grass bodies, white dresses, and outer black robes that enclosed what seemed from a distance like just colorful squares--beautiful. Meaning the dolls did what all beauty does: they made you stop, then drew you in, closer, until you saw what that colorful square was. The doll gave the image a home, a body, and by doing so, it snuck the horror into you; you coudn't turn away, or shut the image out. So the photograph did not desensitize, it stretched the heart open, and at some cost.

But that was only the dolls' effect from the outside. Making the dolls was another thing altogether. Making anything requires care and attention, and making a doll seems to call up a particular sweetness and nurturing. I felt myself, through the making of each body, mothering. Each image, each child, dead or dying—I was mothering their deaths.

And the grasses, too, were alive, swaying, here and there holding drops of rain that shone in the sun until we arrived and cut them down to use. I'd search for long, thin grasses for the head, which now had become her head, or his. I'd harvest this goldenrod here, or that wood aster there, for the child with the large, dark eyes looking up at me from my cloth laid on the gravel. And I was so pleased to find a feast of pasture grasses for that boy, for his arms, which were gone, blown off by God knows what. I swung back and forth between life and death—words I felt viscerally as verbs: life-ing, death-ing—until I couldn't tease the two apart.

But the waves of sadness would flatten periodically into industriousness. We had 16 dolls to make, a number Stubblefield purposely kept high because in a war, "the bodies keep coming." With a mixture of pride and tenderness, I'd place a new plump doll into my bundle and carry it down the road, only to find when I opened the bag again, the grasses were desiccating by the minute, and my babies looked like scarecrows, squished , one against the other. Sorrow would overtake me again and increasingly I felt the burden of the death, deaths I kept carefully making and carrying, because I was the one alive.

A pickup truck slowed down, the driver yelled out, "Get a life," then peeled away. A life. The word shook me in my grief, which had seemed then almost unbearable. But I knew the grief I carried was a gift, a gift from the dolls whose bodies housed the images, which had become mine now and which I held close to my chest. The dolls had given life to my dead.

So the demonstration and the dolls did not end the war in Iraq, and all the years of Bread and Puppet Resurrection Circus demonstrations have not stopped wars, but it seems more important than ever to make a visual stand against business as usual. Can we effect change by presenting a symbol to stand for an option to a wide audience, and gathering support? Dolls telling stories.

Dryer Lint Doll

Pamela: To be made for mass protests

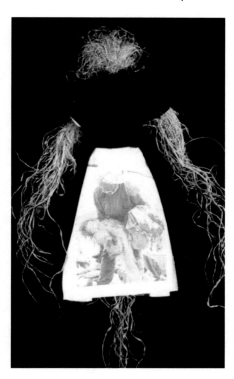

One of the grass dolls with an Iraqi man carrying a dead or dying child on the skirt. Eeo Stubblefield demonstration against the war in Iraq, in NY, 2003.

Annie Hickman: Masks and Costumes

Masks and costumes allow us to transform ourselves almost literally, not that we become someone else. We always have our selves with us, no matter where we go, but we can try on and emphasize or de-emphasize different aspects of our multi-faceted personalities, as children try on different costumes and imitate their parents to see how adults behave. Some people project their bodies right into their dolls and art work, like Lani Gerity using puppets with her patients and now with grandparents and their grandchildren, in a kind of a ritual theater, as part of a larger family story.

Annie Hickman's Transformation came about in one of those a-hah, clicking into place moments, after having grown up with animals, attending art school, working with Sesame Street, dancing, yoga, and making baskets. On stage, before our eyes, she moves to music, gradually donning basket-woven costume parts until she is transformed into a moving cockroach, fly, or centipede. The children in the audience know she's in there, and she brings them into the costuming and the dance, and into greater appreciation for their natural environment, transforming their love of theater and bugs at the same time.

Annie Hickman and some of her masks.

Annie Hickman in Lizard costume

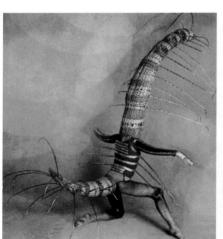

Annie Hickman In Centipede Costume

Bee Happy

A Transformative Family

Arm of the Sea: Transforming Ecological Awareness

"We believe in a theater that moves freely between mythical realms and the daily concerns of existence. We see our mission as one of rediscovering or reinventing archetypal images and stories and presenting them in forms relevant to the day. We search for images that are familiar and commonly understood, yet connected to an ancient, primary source and possessing a quality of mystery that can hold people's attention. Ours is a theater of visual poetry, made by hand, and put to music. It attempts simultaneously to confront the turbulent strata of our historical moment, defend the integrity of the planet's life support systems and suggest the possibilities of personal and social transformation.

"We began in 1982, staging outdoor performances with volunteers in conjunction with the Clearwater, an environmental and cultural organization founded by Pete and Toshi Seeger in New York's Hudson River Valley. These first pieces gave expression to situations within the Hudson ecosystem and explored how the health of the river and the human communities alongside it are interrelated. For visibility and effect we played the main characters with large masks and puppet figures. The stories are told by broad gesture and symbolic action. Live music provided the emotional voicing with text kept minimal and usually sung or chanted by a narrator or chorus. Fifteen years later these same artistic elements, refined by a professional company, continue to be the essential amalgam of our theater.

Arm-of-the-Sea now presents over 100 performances each year at a wide variety of venues throughout the eastern half of the US. Five original works comprise the current repertoire (2004). In an age of pervasive commercialism and homogenization, we strive for something indigenous and home-grown. We draw inspiration from the many traditions of mask and pupped drama, which are rooted in social/political satire as well as religious celebration. Our primary goal is to continue developing a vital theatrical form that takes on present-day quandaries and helps envision, in the sphere of public imagination, a place of resolution and renewal."

Arm-of-the-Sea theater, puppets and performances.

Cindy Pryma: Um Ahmed
Woman II - Freedom   02 January 2005

At the beginning of the War on Terror I felt compelled to write a letter and send it to a variety of newspapers in New South Wales. The following is the gist of what it contained:

> *"But the mothers stayed up to prepare the food for the journey with tender care, and washed their children and packed the luggage and at dawn the barbed wire was full of children's washing hung out in the wind to dry. Nor did they forget the diapers, the toys, the cushions and the hundred other small things which mothers remember and which children always need. Would you not be the same? If you and your child were going to be killed tomorrow, would you not give him to eat today?"* (*If This is a Man* by Primo Levi)

And so I send my children to school and tell them to be nice and play with everyone. And the children watch Playschool and learn to share. And the students are taught right from wrong, to be good, violence is bad. And I remain a woman, a mother, a wife. Restrained by democratic decisions made by Them watching a war destroy the people over There. And my tears are wiped away by a kleenex tissue that is thrown out. And tomorrow morning I will drink a cup of coffee, hang the washing on the Hills Hoist, pack the Wiggles Bag with morning tea and lunch and do the hundred other small things which mothers across Australia remember to do which their children always need. (Letter to the editor, 15 February 2003 by Cynthia Pryma)

When I decided to join the *Woman II* challenge my immediate thoughts focused on the mundane chores that fill my day. I found that my mind wandered to the letter I wrote and how my *mundane* cannot compare to the basics of survival in Darfur. And then the tragedy of the tidal waves in Asia filled the screens.

My doll is a collage of women's faces, all of which are positive figures. The hands stretch up in prayer to a god that might one day fulfill the needs of woman. The barbed wire (a symbol of war, fences, constraint) is used to reach closer to an answer of that prayer. The bound feet symbolize am inability to physically go to help/hold/console/dig for clean water in war torn or natural disaster zones. And the breasts denote a common nurturing among womankind, mother or not.

I have never known tragedy in my life. I can't know the meaning of sorrow. And although my eyes have witnessed, experienced many fears I have never wept. My strength as a woman has never been challenged so I know not its ability to support. I pray for the day when my children's children will be able to see the person before the race or religion.

I found it difficult to place this doll into one theme. However once she was finished she whispered her name and the theme became apparent. *Um* is the Sudanese word for mother. *Ahmed* is my friend who opened my eyes to the civil unrest in Darfur and displays a positive outlook on life in the face of familial despair. To me, his mother is Um Ahmed."

Cyndy Pryma, Australia

Is there a world event that you can relate to your own personal experiences through doll making, as Cindy related the starving mothers' plight in Darfur to taking care of her own children? Sometimes the powerful symbolism of dolls can help a wider audience relate better, too.

More Transformative Doll Making In Practice

Power Icon and Aging
Current issues for me.

"The creative process exposes us to risk, failure, ridicule, misunderstanding. While we shape the work, the work shapes us. If you see crisis as an opportunity, an invitation to personal renewal, then life itself becomes a Creative Process."

— Lucia Capacchione

Setting Ground Rules for a Transformative Project:

Confidentiality is imperative when working in groups. Comments should never be judgemental, ie: "It's pretty," " the head is too big," or "you must be really angry to make something that ugly." The creator can speak for the doll if she/he wishes, "I am round and brown, and grounded in the earth." The doll may not have a specific meaning, or the meaning may not become apparent to the maker until long after completing the piece. A group participant could say, "When I look at this, I feel..." as long as the feelings are clearly owned by the viewer instead of projected onto the creator.

If you are making Transformative dolls in the privacy of your own studio, you may not want to share your most intimate work right away—or ever. Do the work for your own personal growth. You may develop a whole new repertoire of forms and symbols that will make your public art more exciting.

Again, use professional help, too, if the issue is really deep or causing harm in your life.

When making dolls/art in groups or circles we transform both our own and each other's energy and lives. spreading beneficial effects out to our families, all the people with whom we come in contact, and the world. By changing ourselves and the way we live, we transform the wider world, and the universe. The more happiness and connection in the world, the better the chance for peace and living in a way that cherishes all sentient beings (Buddhism). Working in groups has the advantage of increasing the energy for support, being accepted, playing, giving and receiving reinforcement for each individual's worth and the value of each participant's experiences and insights/learning from Crones, gaining the support and validation of the tribe.

Playing within limits/rules and boundaries creates freedom from distractions and old patterns. Use your non-dominant hand to draw, or create questions and responses. Use a technique with which you're not familiar or skilled, to prevent falling back into comfortable patterns. If you are experienced in sewing and face-painting, try wrapping and abstract faces. Use mud, rags, found objects, sticks to stretch your imagination. You'll be amazed at the powerful results.

Don't allow your Inner Critic to have a say. Be a child, play making dolls with a child, play like a child, reconnect with your inner child. Follow your First thoughts rather than censoring with your Second thoughts. Work and create ceremonies to forget your Self and watch to see what emerges. Whatever you do is okay. Years from now look back at what you've made and see these milestones as tracks along your way.

Different processes will work better for different people. I resist hard materials that require pounding or drilling, and now I use them for construction with Apoxie Sculpt. Incorporating a found object forces me to stretch my ingenuity, and gets me out of comfortable design solutions.

When you are dealing with a challenging topic, a material that is unfamiliar could help to express your frustration with your subject...or just make it impossible to proceed. You may find yourself expressing new art forms in order to express what is inside you.

People/your students or audience are ready to deal with different topics at different times in their own personal development, so don't force it. On the other hand, many experience the strongest resistance just before a break through. In working with students and clients, you will develop a sensitivity to how much pushing anyone can handle.

Giving birth to your past may be painful and difficult at first—a strong aversion to one stage of the process may signify that something important is being born. An opening may follow.

"The only way out is through," I kept reminding myself while I was working on re-establishing my life as an individual of value after 17 year of being belittled in my marriage. Later I saw how easy it was for me to fall into that destructive trap again in a job for a man who used his intelligence to blame others for his own failings. That one only lasted four months—one does learn to recognize subtle patterns of abuse and to create a trusted support system for reality checks when needed.

ALAC
Money doll with gaping hole, never to be completely filled. Unknown Artist from files

Judith Scott was a mentally-retarded person who created sculptures with amazing presence by wrapping stolen objects with yarn. I saw her work displayed at the American Visionary Art Museum in Baltimore, MD.

Sentinel Series
2008

Unfortunately the boss/employee dynamic can lead to abuse, and it's often a difficult relationship to leave for financial reasons, making it even more important not to absorb and internalize the abuse.

Learn to listen with opened ears to your students. Other people may use different frames of reference that may seem foreign until you translate them into your own language. Do the same for yourself when what comes out of you seems strange or disturbing.

Choose a technique that is comfortable in order to more easily concentrate on what you want to express—or use an unfamiliar technique in order to help let go of inhibitions. Parent yourself and your students by giving yourself as much permission to be creative, as much support and encouragement as you would give your children. Although much of what forms a personality happens in the first four years, learning and growing never stop. You CAN re-program yourself, if you are motivated to do so. The more work you create, the more ideas you'll have for additional pieces. Some topics call for multiple art works to explore them fully and bring them to manageable size and importance.

Try different types of exercises: wrapping, drawing, sewing, paper versus cloth, working alone versus in a group. You need to invent a new art form to express what is in you.

Our culture/school system teaches the suppression of emotional and creative urges. It is easy to control those who don't understand their feelings. You must unlearn that. Take baby steps to start. Forget your sense of Self and watch what emerges and evolves in your work. The creations are tracks left along the path of progress, what you make is not YOU. If what you see is disturbing, remember that the whole range of human feelings is part of each of us, part of our legacy as human beings. That is why parents and society have a responsibility to Civilize children's wildest natures, at the same time maintaining their individuality and creativity. We may have to unlearn some overbearing lessons of civilization and suppression from our youth as we come in closer touch with our instinctive sub-conscious sides. Perhaps some raised on constant phone and computer entertainment will have to develop the habits of discipline and focus required by creative work. Start with simple projects for them.

Like a broom sweeping away dust and residue, creation acts as a purification of what has accumulated in the life of the psyche. When repressed feelings appear in concrete form a vibrant energy floods the body and you feel relieved because you don't have to stand guard any more," write Michele Cassou and Steward Cublen in Life, Paint, and Passion.

Don't be afraid that if you get rid of the pain, your art will suffer. Transformative work is a life-long process. There will be a host of new ideas where the old repetitive tape loops of hurt were previously blocking your expressive work.

Creativity involves looking, listening, and being with an open mind. Don't worry about needing artistic angst in order to envision new work. There will still be plenty of up and down days. Use dolls as containers for feelings and ideas. Try a box for a body. The repetitive process of examining your issues in different ways will bring about new meanings and insights. Your exorcism will come in stages, with looping returns to earlier stages, not with a huge, exploding epiphany.

The questions of What is Quality, What is Art? These can be ignored in this process, since the purpose of the work is for the creator alone. Whatever you make is perfect for this process.

I admire the skill involved in art work, but I am Drawn to work that shows the hand, thought, and feeling of the maker. The works provide pleasure in their execution and pleasure in their contemplation. They are created from energy and arouse energy in response. One develops personal symbolism and themes, as well as Universal Jungian themes. The Flow comes from being so deeply immersed in the piece that boundaries between the maker and the work disappear. When my work touches others and calms my interior churning, I am satisfied.

The presence of Judith Scott's dolls (p. 117), some as tall as people, inspired my Sentinel series, as did the tall ranks of evergreens when I first drove into the Evergreen State.

Sentinel 8
From the series in 2008. The tall evergreens when I first drove into WA to live were Sentinels to me.

Breaking Out Of My Box
2010 12″ I've done a number of pieces on this theme.

119

Sara Austin on the Question of Dolls as Art

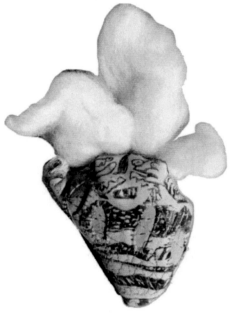

"Hearing the expression Art Dolls causes me to wonder Are Dolls Art? Tell anyone that you make dolls and the image of the wide-eyed porcelain beautiful doll is conjured. I certainly didn't take Doll making seriously when I first started making them many years ago. Dolls for me were a diversion from years of painting and drawing. One day I happened to see some intriguing fabric dolls in a gallery and thought it would be fun to make one. One turned into some, and some turned into many, as my love of fabric and three-dimensional forms grew stronger. In order for the dolls to be considered totally original I felt, the fabric should all be hand dyed and hand printed, and later on hand painted. i still feel that way, and like the process of building up layers of color with dye, printing, painting, and dye removal. The fabric is treated like a painting and then cut to make the shapes for the figure.

"Doll making came to me at a time in my life when I needed to make them. I was learning about mythology, reading the stories of Persephone and other myths and images would come into my head that I had to create. These were my first three-dimensional figures. There were faces in the front and back. I felt that they should be able to sit and stand, like real peple, and that every surface should be covered, to say something from every point of view. It became a passion. I made quite a few dolls about my own past and issues I was dealing with.

" I don't know if any of the dolls I've made are Art or not. It doesn't matter at this point. Now that I've made so many, taught classes to others in creating their own dolls, made and sold endless dolls and doll patterns, each with their own meanings and technical information, I feel that I've helped open a wonderful world to others. When I look at them I still wonder if these things are ART. the doll concept still has the stigma of craft and I don't know if that will ever go away. I do know that the history of dolls is fascinating, and I'd like to continue learning and teaching this craft."

When we make dolls for our own Transformation, it doesn't really matter whether the world thinks of them as Art.

Sara Austin Dolls

Judy Dahlin: Transformation/Blessings

"Last year I made a figure from fabric, sticks, wire, paper clay, herbs, and birch bark. I wrote messages on the birch bark rectangles handing down from the arms. When I saw these wonderful Asian papers, I wanted to use the same idea in a different way, so this is the result. Each blessing hanging from the arms contains secret messages, thoughts, dreams, and ideas."

"The materials were : Coffee stir sticks, paper, acrylic, waxed linen, bells, and a face stamp I designed"

Judy Dahlin

Use a simple paper or cloth body shape and hang your messages or blessings from the stick

Margaret McGuinness: Recovery

**Woman Warrior of
Recovery: Honesty (Detail)**

Margaret McGuinness

(rear view)

Shaman

Margaret McGuinness Canvas,
sculpey, wood, paint.

"Dolls were always more than what they appeared to be whenever I recall my life as a child. They offered solace, fought demons, were absolute friends, never leaving me. I began making dolls very early, as I could sew by age 5. Fast forward, now I make dolls to celebrate my own and my women friends' recovery. The Women Warriors of Recovery doll series celebrate the message of the 12 Steps of Alcoholics Anonymous of Honesty, Openness and Willingness. Recovery through attraction, hope, and the courage to carry the message of the twelve steps of AA provide each a new way of life.

"I believe that what we make in art, with others, connects us to something greater than ourselves. Jung refers to this as "the collective unconscious." Elders in tribal groups from across the globe connect to the "ancestors." Dolls have a long history of being "emissaries," carrying the magic, the wish/desire, to this greater collective and manifesting the message in some way to its maker. Dolls are also used as "stand-ins," representing a human for specific purposes. The wrapped dolls I create and teach were first presented to me at a workshop I attended by African-American artist Riua Akinshegun, called "Dolls That Carry You Home, " in 1995. The subsequent workshops I present, "The Doll as Healing Image" facilitate resiliency necessary for recovery, as it represents hope, fostering resiliency.

"The process of creating a wrapped doll facilitates transformation as the artist, through repetitive steps, embarks on an active meditation, opening the mind to greater awareness allowing for enhanced self-expression. As the image emerges, the artist responds, and the dance of creation transforms humble scraps into active engagement with the "other." Through each artist's eyes, the doll has become more than what they started with, stands for what they need at this time/place, and allows for response, always providing what is needed by the creator.

"I have provided workshops for health professionals, women cancer survivors, children who have lost a family member to cancer, and local artists."

122

(Rear View)

Woman Warrior of Recovery
Margaret McGuinness

Margaret M. McGuinness MA, Med, ATR-BC

"I have worked as an art therapist in Michigan since 1997, mostly with adolescents in residential treatment and adults with Traumatic Brain Injury. I currently have a small private practice working with children with attachment trauma. I have co-written chapters for two art therapy books with a colleague on our work with TBI and bullying. McGuinness, M. & Schnur, K., Art Therapy, Creative Apperception, and Rehabilitation from Traumatic Brain Injury, in Malchiodi, C., (ed,). Art Therapy and Healthcare, Guilford Press, NY. In manuscript: McGuinness, M. & Schnur, K., Bullying, Trauma, and Creative Arts Interventions, in Malchiodi, C., (ed.), Creative Interventions for Traumatized Children, rev, Guilford Pub., NY Due 2015."

Healer
Margaret McGuinness 20″
Wrapped doll

Lani Gerity: Art Therapist Using Dolls and Puppets

Paper Doll Self With Doll
Lani Gerity

Quiet Renewal
Lani Gerity
Daily collage on FaceBook.

"I worked many years in New York City as an art therapist, watching, celebrating, and delighting in the Transformative power of art making, but it was always a kind of second-hand celebration. During these years what stood out was the changing and unfolding expression of body image in dolls and puppets. This was a magical activity, using three-dimensional doll making materials in a way that restored for the individual his or her own sense of self. Over and over I saw a struggle and resolution of early childhood trauma in the creation of story, puppets, and dolls. Over the years it became very clear to me that it was the creative process that was unlocking the possibility for the sense of self to achieve new levels of integration and grown. I saw my role as being a support of creative effort, an ally to the creative aspect of the self, while the individual's own art-making process worked towards ameliorating and Transforming self and life.

"One survivor told me that the day she started creating a head of a person who was very dear to her, something magical happened. She said she felt a deep connection to a mysterious part of herself. She could put everything into this head she was working on—her love, her anger, her fears—and what emerged was a thing of beauty. She felt validated by this head that she could touch, feel, and look at. She could see that it was good, it reflected back to her a very deep sense of self-worth and even self-love. She was learning to cherish and love herself again.

"Well you can only work so many years in this way before you start to wonder what this unfolding process might be like from the inside out. I could try being a support to my own creative effort, become an ally to the creative aspect of the self, watch my own doll and puppet making process lead me toward an ameliorating and transforming self and life. Since then, I've moved to Nova Scotia where I make dolls and puppets and lead creativity workshops of all kinds, for all ages, and in all sorts of conditions. My life has been turned inside out in exciting and delightful ways, since I decided to follow this path.

"The self-portrait puppet and doll were created with an old childhood photo, some heavy water color paper, stamps yarns, brads, markers, and a photocopy machine. The feelings that were awakened in this process were of wanting to find more ways to cherish this creation, creative process, and creator. I wanted to create a heart, to make the hair as wildly colorful as possible, and mostly to give her a doll to hold. The only thing I can say really is to try it for yourself. It is so much fun, and the possibilities seem endless. I am now moving on to other family members, finding old photos and playing with them in this same gentle Transformative way."

Enchantment
Lani Gerity
Daily collage on FaceBook.

From Lani's Blog 2015:

Gretchen Miller challenged me to participate in an art chain, to post art every day for five days over on FaceBook. Well, I've been doing that for a couple of years now, but I thought why not go through my archives and see what resonates the most right now. So what I discovered is that creating art every day as part of my daily practice, has made me happier, braver, and more resilient. Each day along with the art there will be a little text of encouragement, a reminder to engage in creative and meditative practices, to remember that we can imagine new, richer possibilities, to bring more color into the world, and to allow the daily practice to be a door that opens on to all sorts of possibilities.

With my fairly comprehensive background in art therapy, masters and doctorate in the discipline, I keep coming back to the simple idea that by making art, and doing our very best, we learn to feel deeply happy, to pay attention to our life and the things that matter, we actually learn to love who we are a little more every day.

1. Develop a daily art practice
2. Always look for the good and if you can't find it, create it
3. Clean up after yourself
4. Create art with your monsters
5. Be curious (don't worry, we can never know everything)
6. Practice kindness as much as possible (it's always possible)
7. Have adventures
8. Love what you do
9. Share what you love, share the good stuff

Kindness
Lani Gerity
Daily collage on FaceBook.

Karen Shelton Interviews Non-Traditional Doll Makers

Diapers
Karen Shelton 11″
Collage and writing

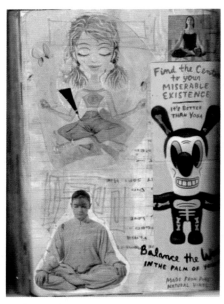

Yoga Collage
Karen Shelton

Karen Shelton: *"The reasons that doll makers give to explain why they make dolls are as varied as their handcrafted dolls. This art form is apparently an outlet for an entire range of human expression. Yet there is a common thread: doll making seems to answer an a ancient call for those who hear it."*

Sunny: *"I believe the dolls's origins to be primitive and basic in nature, and that the concept of the doll was born from a basic need to explore one's identity in relation to the world."*

Jeannette: *"Humans naturally want someone or something to love and to be loved back. Dolls can give a very pure love in our minds, like animals, because we believe that they care nothing for our faults and love us no matter what. Parenthood is also an instinct, and dolls allow humans from an early age to nurture that instinct."*

Missy: *"We were given the doll and told of that ancestor and it kept their memories alive. I took some bits and pieces of a relative's old clothes and made a small quilt for my daughter and her dolls. It means more because it contains scraps of their essence."*

Carol: *"People's inherent instinct of wanting to see human form in all things has given them the ability to perceive a rock or a stick as resembling a human. It's all a matter of perception."*

Several doll makers were asked to describe their compulsion to create these representations of the human form.

Jeannette: *"I heard about a culture that makes its own dolls, so I tried it. The beginning was not impressive, but I liked having a friend to carry around to class. I mostly make dolls because I enjoy creating something. I suppose I have a bit of a Frankenstein complex."*

Carol: *"There is a bit of a god complex associated with the creation of a little person. One day in the late 1980's I was working on a series of paintings of clowns and I really had the desire to make something three-dimensional. I had an old black and white sweater out of which I cut the shape of a clown and stitched it together. I thought it was the most amazing feeling to be able to hold in my hand some art that I had created that was not a piece of paper."*

Mizzy: *"There has never been a time when I found myself NOT creating. Maybe I need to make dolls, to leave part of myself beyond my lifespan, to have something to remind MY grandchildren about me, just as I hold dear the small memoirs of my ancestors."*

Holly: *"I started doll making around July of 2000 when I went doll hunting for my own collection. I couldn't find anything that seemed to fit me and then decided, why not make my own? I make dolls out of my fascination with them and my love for collecting. It feels good to know that others are collecting what I make and to know that I am creating something that can evoke many different reactions from people. Some are repelled, some attracted, which has always been my own mixed reaction to dolls."*

Conjoined Twins
Karen Shelton Fabric

Diane: *"I have loved dolls since I was a little girl They always brought me such happiness, and now that I am grown up, I think it's great to make dolls that bring happiness to others! Until I was eight I was an only child, so my dolls would entertain me for hours. I was in my own little world when playing with my dolls. I design and sew clothing and one day just decided to give doll making a try, mostly because I fell in love with other dolls people had made. I also have a doll collection of my own and thought it would be fun to make some for other people to collect."*

Karen: *"Creating the dolls and working on them is just my way of playing with them. It is not much different from what I did with my dolls as a child. I think of my dolls as my offspring and I consider doll making to be Play Therapy. I also have a magpie-like desire to collect shiny, colorful things, which is as much fun as making the dolls."*

Baby Sitter
Karen Shelton 11″ Collage

Sunny: *"It is my way of assessing who I am in relation to my vision of the world, my collected experiences, hopes, and fears."*

Jeanette: *"For children it is a way of trying out situations and roles, and it prepares them for the real thing when they are older. For me, as a twenty-year-old, play is an escape and it allows me to be whatever I want, have as many friends as I want, and to just be in control of a fantasy world. Play can give a fresh perspective on problems and perhaps while we play our subconscious, as it does in sleep, may provide a solution."*

Sunny: *"Creating a doll is an excuse to express parts of my personality and explore what they are and why they are there"*

127

Frog Hand
Karen Shelton 11″ Paper

Doll
Karen Shelton 10″
Paper, lace, photos

Holly: "*Play is very important to children and adults. Most people just don't see it. We're too busy worrying about everything else we have to deal with and we don't spend enough time cherishing the things we did as children Take your dolls out, clean them up, dress them, pose them, or play any way you know how, but don't ever forget what's important in life and what really matters. Believe it or not, what matters most is not how much money was on your W2's last year or how perfect your car looks as you cruise down the road. If you don't know what's important, pick up an old doll and remember what it was like to sit under an oak tree on a sunny day, confessing your secrets to her silent lips, and feeling as if life could not be more sublime.*"

Karen: *On the surface, dolls appear to be simple playthings or collectibles. However, there is a deeper aspect to doll making that leads to spiritual or even physical healing.*"

Mizzy: "*Doll making takes away the day to day stress of my family and the mistakes that haunt me. I get depressed, but I can pick up a paintbrush or a sewing needle and I begin to lose myself in another place. It's as if I have too much 'me' inside my body and I feel too completely full of emotion; so I can go off on a wall with some paint and get it out and give it to the wall, so I can live there instead of inside me.*

Sunny: "*In my life-long battle for self esteem, I've found that creation in any form has been a safe way for me to declare my right to exist. With creation we are taking up some space in the world with something that says, 'Look at me! Acknowledge me!'*

Carol: "*I can work out my problems and express my feelings through a doll. On days when I am angry the dolls come out with facial features that convey that emotion. Doll making has made me calmer and not as angry. Sometimes after I finish a doll it makes me laugh—the greatest feeling! With art I have been able to drag myself out of the mire of self pity and depression.*"

Karen: "*However limited or flexible your definition of a doll is, allow yourself some private time with these representations of the human race. Some unexpected questions may arise that you would like to ask them. If you are fortunate to be able to converse with dolls, you may just find the solutions to all the problems of the universe.*"

Liz Pearce

Liz was suggested by her daughter, Julie Voss. I am impressed by Liz's extensive website, varied doll creations, and poetry. I'm especially touched that she thanked elinor peace bailey and Me for inspiring her—my life is complete! Seriously, you won't regret spending time on her site: www.heartfeltdolls.weebly.com. Please visit Liz's website for dolls on depression, divorce, and environmental destruction.

Hair Today
Liz Pearce

AN INVITATION by Liz Pearce

At 52, I encountered a major change in my life.
Slowly, I honoured the call to become a doll maker.
Whenever I was amongst fabric artists or immersed in my doll making,
I found I was energized, excited, joyful.
I wondered if this was an invitation to share the intimacy and persistence of divine love
through my dolls.
For me, doll making is contemplative.
My attention is focused.
I am surrounded by possibilities.
I immerse myself ... and a new doll is birthed.
With each stage of this process, God's love enfolds me.
With each stitch, I feel more closely stitched to the divine.
Doll making becomes a wordless communion with God.

**Terri and Francie:
Friends for the Journey**
Liz Pearce

Just Checkin
Liz Pearce

**Pearl and Glam at the
Mammogram Slam**
Liz Pearce

Transformative Dolls Dealing with Aging, Death and Loss

Grief

2010 12″ Collage the style inspired by a class with Anne Grgich

Guardian Doll for the Critically Ill
Andrea Cooley He holds the basket filled with birds and a small curled up figure.

In the over ten years since I wrote the first version of this book, I have learned a lot, taught, made art, suffered some, moved many miles, studied Buddhism, and developed a greater appreciation for a widening range of concerns. As always, I'm working from my own self out, to explore the issues of aging and death—and I was able to vicariously experience the struggles of others as I returned to practicing occupational therapy in order to Be Able To retire from the world of work and worries about money at the relatively young age of 68.

I heard recently that Baby Boomers equate aging and death. We have been on top of the heap for longer than the generations ahead of us, and have bought into the youth culture we created in our growing reluctance to give up control—from the last gasp of the self-satisfied prosperous white male in politics, to endless grannie face lifts or Botox injections.

I am not immune. My first year and a half of retirement/All Art, All the Time were spent mourning, divesting, feeling guilty that my time was no longer eaten up by the concerns of making a living, and to a great extent in mourning and fear. Fear of losing independence, control, eyesight, mobility, cognition, and most of all having to amend the self image I had been carefully constructing over the last 68 years. Of course none of us are the same person we were twenty years ago—or even one second ago, and we do have to make space on this planet for those who are rapidly coming up behind us.

Being older is painful—mentally and physically. Being dependent and un-acknowleged might be the worst for me. Where are those who will want to listen to our stories? Where are those who remember us when we were smooth and sexy? What is the proper balance between working to prolong health and being ridiculous? When I was working in health care, in nursing homes and hospitals I saw people who felt they had no quality of life and just wanted to die. I don't want to be one of them. Transformative doll/art making with the elderly to honor the past could be valuable—we identify with our memories.

Iris: A movie, very old very rich ladies dressing as an art form, long skinny legs and lots of jewelry. Why not Express Oneself in whatever medium she can afford? My 100 Hot Flash Women series: "Ordinary" women immortalized in paint. People who are who they are—character reflected in faces and dress. Wake up to the night, regrets, vengeance, creativity, fears, painting. Creating a reason for What Is. Repeating stories—Like a piece of poetry jotted on a scrap of paper—my life concerns. Could I embrace the wrinkly sac of skin if I can keep the brain that imagines and ponders? A new territory, indeed!

"Fearing aging is about fearing death, or infirmity, or a progressive lack of independence. And maybe it's about vanity. Of course it's about vanity. But it's also about control—about how much of it we have over our own bodies, our own lives, our futures. In other words this whole aging thing is loaded. So when I lie about my age, I'm not just fiddling with numbers. I'm giving expression to my own fears of illness and dependence."

— Lauren Kessler

"Oh my god, what if you wake up some day and you're 65, or 75 and you never got your memoir or novel written; or you didn't go swimming in warm pools and oceans all those years because your thighs were jiggly and you had a nice big comfortable tummy; or you were just so strung out on perfectionism and people-pleasing that you forgot to have a big juicy creative life, of imagination and radical silliness and staring off into space like when you were a kid? It's going to break your heart. Don't let this happen."

— Anne Lamott

Stay with the Journey
2014 14" Mixed items, Road Trip.

Surveying a New Territory
2015 9" New fabric/mixed media series on learning to accept the changes of aging and embrace the opportunities. The figure is surveying new territory from a distance right now.

Additional Projects: Amulets and Small Icons

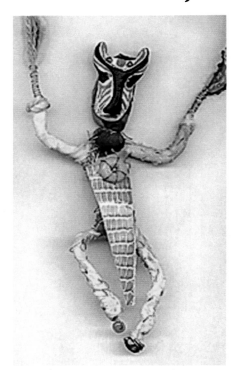

Small dolls and amulets: Remember the power of the process of making a concrete representation of your fears and then transforming that doll, and your fears, into something more positive. "Whatever doesn't kill me makes me stronger." Neitzsche.

Here are some samples, for which you will need a very small turning tool—or use felt or Ultrasuede with outside seams, or do a tiny wrapped stick doll. Use a very short stitch length so the fabric won't unravel and lots of beads and embellishment.

There is something very comforting about a hand or pocket-sized talisman. Make one for a friend who is going through chemo therapy...or a job interview. Add an affirmation inside and significant charms.

CHALLENGES:

• Make a doll or mixed media project that represents that you have already experienced with Life Issues.

• Make a miniature healing icon or amulet for yourself or someone else to focus healing energy, remembering not to impose your own prejudices about outcomes.

• Be an active participant in your own healing and learn as much as possible about what conventional medicine can offer, as well as alternative healing methods, which conventional medicine is slow to accept.

• Take care of your health every day—it's one of your most precious attributes. Nurturing yourself takes more time as you get older. Luckily you may have more time then to do it.

• Listen very carefully to those you are helping—what do they REALLY want?

• Accept what you can't change, learn the lessons.

AMULET

There are numberless simple body shapes and types that you can use in your Transformative Doll Making and Art. My Graphic Grannies Comics, which I publish intermittently online are visualizations around my concerns about aging and the future of our planet. This book can't fit into just one category of doll making or therapy. Now there are many, many more books on creativity and using a wide range of 2-D and 3-D figure forms for patient treatment as well as for individual exploration and personal stretching.

I am including a selection of email comments from the online versions of my class because you will see the same topics coming up again and again. I tried to hang back and let the students respond to each other's questions/statements. Disappointing families and marriages came up again and again, and there was some very insightful discussion on forgiveness and release. Groups can make very useful venues for doing this work. As you see, the feedback that one is not alone in experiencing these problems and support for dissipating the power of the old baggage is spread around the group.

No Exit

2004 12" Paper cup, model magic, collage, wire staple, fimo, feather. I made this in a Barb Kobe workshop when I was deciding to leave my last relationship (I left 5 months later). I hope that in the future I can work to change relationships while I am participating in them, instead of waiting until I am totally fed up and then running far away We must be sufficiently aware to notice when we are in pain and then feel justified in addressing the pain.

No Exit (Detail)

Tiny Cloth Icon

Worry Dolls

Very powerful statements can be made with simple, repetitive forms. Since the intention is the important aspect of Transformative Doll Making, repeating the intention over and over, as in folding paper cranes, increases the amount of time focusing on the desired outcome.

Simple doll forms may be cut from paper or fabric—adjust the patterns to meet your needs. Look at Indigenous shapes for inspiration.

The Worry dolls are a good opportunity to Bless and Release the obsessive fears presented on the nightly news... or assist a client or yourself to customize and minimize—bring them down to manageable size. Burn them.

The Prayer Angels use magazine or hand-written phrases for good wishes, strung together on a ribbon. Celebrate a triumph or help heal.

PRAYER ANGEL

WORRY DOLL SHIRT

WORRY DOLL TOP

WORRY DOLL LEGS

Worry Dolls/Prayer Dolls

Cut patterns from cardboard, collage larger shapes with glue stick. Then trace around the patterns and cut, add appropriate phrases.

Love Thyself Doll

Love Thyself
We can never have or give too many reminders to love ourselves and shower ourselves and others with blessings.

Love Thyself
Use your own face here as a photo transfer, or the abstract one. Makes a good gift.

Cut 2
Trace, sew, clipcurves
Leave bottom open A to B
With right sides together,
Sew to base, leaving a wide
opening at the back
Insert stiff cardboard and
weight, slip stitch closed

A   Leave open   ©Pamela
2012   B

Leave Open

Cut a piece of stiff
cardboard a little
smaller — add that
and a weight (big
washer or stone)
Inside

A   B

Blessings Doll in Cloth or Paper

HEAD

Pamela

HANDS
BDoll

BLESSING
DOLL
ARMS
Fabric-Cut 4
Paper-Cut 2

Pamela

For Paper Cut 2
Cut Door in top layer

DOOR for | PAPER
DOLL

FOLD

FOLD

BLESSING DOLL
BODY

Cut 2

For fabric
Sew on traced
lines-leave
an opening
to turn &
Stuff

Pamela

You may want to make blessings dolls—a focus or intent—for yourself, a loved one, this beautiful green and blue planet that we inhabit. Through learning to cherish ourselves, the love spreads—and who knows?

Blessing Doll
Paper above and fabric below.

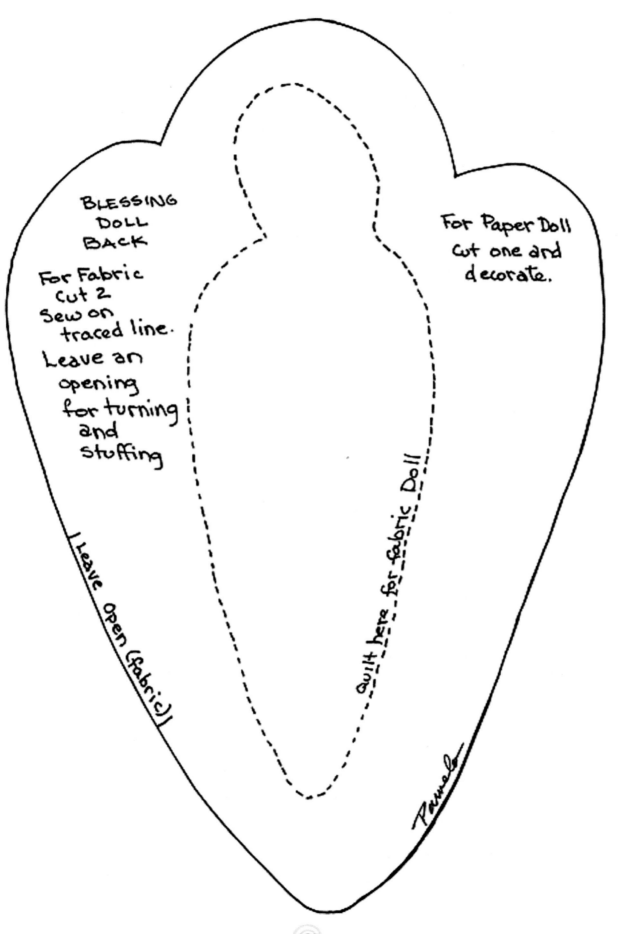

BLESSING
DOLL
BACK

For Fabric
Cut 2
Sew on
traced line.

Leave an
opening
for turning
and
stuffing

For Paper Doll
Cut one and
decorate.

Leave open (fabric)

Quilt here for Fabric Doll

Pamela

Comments from Transformative Dollmaking Online - 1

"Wow! This class just got more intense for me. I was having fun piddling around with the paper dolls last week—but this project is really challenging me to think more—and to be more honest with myself. I've started my stick doll and I've been journaling like crazy with all the ideas and conflicts it's bringing forth."

— L

"This has been a rough week for me and my first doll is in my head—I see it so clearly! I just can't bring myself to give myself the time I so desperately need and deserve to start this one simple step. I want this to be fun and exciting and a personal journey—it just seems to be a little scary right now to start."

— T

"In a class like this one, I think that the things we create only in our heads can be as helpful as the stuff we actually bring into the world. Maybe it will be helpful to write a couple of quick notes in your journal about how you see your doll in your head, just to hold onto the idea until you can make time to work on her"

— L

"We are playing in the biggest and best sandbox in the world, and we are all here together, recognizing and giving validation and support to each other."

— P

"Went on my twig search, but wound up with only two: a wonderfully-distorted torso with legs and a rather grotesque head with two twisted arms. She'd be about 17 inches tall. Not what I intended but she's insisting on being made. Don't want to cover up all the great dents, bumps, and fissures on the torso and head so will paint her red."

— J

"Again and again: try to resist comparing anything of yours unfavorably to anything that anyone else does. We come with what we have. We share and learn. It's not a competition—don't let your gremlins make it into one."

— P

"I read your comment about rejection from your mother. I've been dealing with mother rejection all my life and though I believe I have released myself from her I still find it hard to understand. I was the first born, an unwanted pregnancy in 1949. I have three siblings. My youngest brother was born in 1966 and was also unwanted. I still cannot forgive myself for not taking a stand when she slapped him around in his high chair. I was 17 then and no support from my father and siblings."

— G

Comments from Transformative Dollmaking Online - 2

"When I am working with women with 'MOM stuff' I ask them to remove the 'Mother' label and look at their mother as just a WOMAN. Sometimes it helps to understand their actions when we view them as just a troubled woman. These women who are our mothers did not have the benefit of self awareness books, support groups, therapy, psychiatric medications, etc. They did not speak of depression (post partum depression didn't even have a name), anxiety, sexual or physical abuse. They put on their lipstick and apron, stuck the pot roast in the oven and smiled. Then they fell apart in private (my mother sat on the floor in the closet and cried)."

— H

"I have found my secret is in letting go—over and over. That is me. I want to get back to doll making and love the idea of exploring ourselves with the class—there is so much to know! I do journal and have been working with The Artist Way, writing 3 pages a day and tearing them up."

— M

"Usually for inspiration I clean up my sewing room and just seeing and touching all the fabric, beads, feathers, bones, buttons, etc. sparks an idea. I was in the middle of the worst time I ever had with one of my children—drugs—and I made this doll with words written all over it—all of the feelings I was having and no face.

— N

"I agree with H. When I view my mother as a troubled person, it really helps. I too have a strained relationship with my mother, but over the years this is what I have come to know:

1. I cannot change the past; I have only today, this moment in time I am losing my mother to old age and possibly Alzheimer's so this one is really important to me.

2. I cannot change anyone, I can only change myself.

3. My thoughts are MY thoughts, NO ONE creates my thoughts; someone's actions or words may cause me to have certain thoughts, based on my beliefs and past experiences but I choose my own thoughts.

4. I choose to believe that my mother did (and is doing) the best she can based on what she believes, her past experiences and circumstances in life.

5. I choose to be happy, rather than right."

— H

Comments from Transformative Doll Making Online - 3

"Sometimes when the personal scary stuff is made concrete in art work it loses some of its power to frighten us. Our US culture often seems to find real things like death, anger, poverty, incest, abuse, disease very frightening. If we acknowledge that these things do exist, can't we deal with their fall out more effectively? I find myself re-inacting my abusive marriage in different permutations again in work and relationships. At least now I can recognize the symptoms sooner and take steps for change. This is a Process. One never stops working, but then it is all so Interesting!"

— P

"I turned 50 this year and decided it's time to start addressing my own needs and desires. My husband was in the military for 24 years and I spent that time focusing my time and energy on raising our kids and moving around with his career. It was a great experience—not always positive—but I wouldn't trade it. Now that we've settled in a civilian community and our kids are out on their own adventures I'm having a hard time building a fulfilling life for myself. I've applied to the University of Kansas to study textile design—but I'm scared that I'm not talented enough and that I'll be embarrassed by my attempts. I'm hoping this class will help me work through some of those issues!"

— L

"Fantasy caregiver is a wonderful term and I am going to make me one. My parents would not acknowledge that my ex was abusive—even when my dad had to take me to the emergency room. They assumed it was my fault—I guess because I had been such a difficult child to raise. I probably wouldn't have been so difficult for someone else, but who knows. When I was in the process of leaving my ex-husband, my dad said to me, If you leave ___, that will be the end of him." Nice, huh. I don't talk about this usually, because I don't want people to feel sorry for me. I hate that. Anyway, both of my parents are dead and so is my ex-husband. He spent several years in prison after shooting his girlfriend in the back. I was very, very lucky, I know that. And that is part of what drives me to create. I have had some close calls, but I am still here, and I want to be the best that I can be. It's like paying a debt, I guess. I give most of my dolls away, because they make people happy."

— N

Comments from Transformative Doll Making Online - 4

"My husband tried to break my spine, but luckily he didn't do any permanent damage. It took me 20 years of doll making, journaling, therapy and lots of work to forgive him for being who he was. It's NOT OK under any circumstances for people to gratuitously hurt each other. The only people we're really responsible, besides minor children, is ourselves."

— P

"My main problem is confidence in the work I do, although getting better working in a group and exhibiting, I still have more ideas than projects that actually get started—for fear of failure more often than not. Today I sat down and started cutting out pictures and thinking of the project at hand, I have found it really useful to think about what I do and don't like and put this into   images"

— J

"Thanks for the advice to try using inexpensive supplies instead of our best stash stuff. I didn't realize how much I was holding back from getting started until I read that post and realized that I was also reluctant to "waste" any of my good stuff. I ended up using an old grocery bag and I had a lot of fun just letting myself go without any worries about what came of it."

— L

"I did a lot of thinking about "forgiving" while cutting the grass for three hours. I grew up in a family that appeared normal but in retrospect was quite dysfunctional. I have no relationship with my parents and siblings today. My father is passive, my mother domineering and critical although she likes to pretend otherwise. I had the perfect qualifications for a disastrous first marriage—some physical abuse but mainly emotional. At 35 I started to think that here i was a professional making a good wage and my ex was in control of my pay cheque. It only took 14 years for me to figure out that wasn't right. The concept of forgiving people like my parents and ex husband doesn't seem possible for me. How do you forgive people who hurt you so deeply and leave scars? Aren't they responsible for their actions? "

— G

"The hardest person to forgive has been myself, for stupidly getting caught in a terrible situation and for staying trapped in it for so long. I lost confidence in my own judgement."

— T

Comments from Transformative Doll Making Online - 5

"Forgiveness has nothing to do with the person you are forgiving. It is for your benefit not theirs. When I am working on this issue with abused women, I don't use the term Forgiveness but rather Release. When you can release the anger, hurt, person, situation, etc, you are able to step outside of it and say, 'this no longer defines me or has power over me.' It isn't about who is right or wrong, or saying what happened was OK, it is about laying it down and walking on without the burden of unforgiveness. Unforgiveness is one of the lowest level emotions there is, right down there with shame, guilt, fear, and anger. From an energy perspective (which is what I work with) these emotions suck the life right out of you. Forgiveness, or releasing unforgiveness is for your benefit, something you do for yourself, for YOUR healing."

— H

"Learning to trust our own selves can take a lot of trial and error, becoming more sure as we go along. Don't let fear stop you from trying the things that may release you. When not sure about which direction to take with a project start two the same way, then let each go off in its own direction. Come back to this material again and again to see which way you use it."

— P

"More often than not we never get that apology form the person who has wronged us. It is a process to release and lay it down. True release happens when you can look at the offense, person, feeling, with gratitude for the lessons learned from the experience. It is work to get there but it is when you know you have healed that part of your spirit."

— H

"It's been helpful for me to view emotions like clouds—always changing. I think one of the devastating aspects of depression is the feeling that this state will never end, which for me led to suicidal thinking. The concept of "release" is very appropriate, but it's important to remember that this is a process and to maintain compassion for yourself. Deciding to let your long-held anger go is a start. Develop compassion and forgiveness for yourself first."

— J

"Don't forget to celebrate your positive transforming life events as well as the negative ones. Several friends are caring for parents going through the dying process and finding joy as well as sorrow in helping with the transition and sharing an intimate experience with family members."

— P

Graphic Grannies (Ongoing)
Combining collage and drawing, I work out political/personal ideas

Contributors

My heartfelt thanks go out to each contributor to this book. I have found that the contact information for some is no longer easily available on the Web, so I entered the last known address.

Adams, Christine, p 74, 75   Uncommon.threads@erols.com

Arm of the Sea, p107   armofthesea.org

Austin, Sara, p 80, 81, 114   www.facebook.com/saralunafiber

Blair, Arlinka, p 16, 17   www.facebook.com/

Blakeslee, Mermer, p 104, 105   mermer@citilink.net

Briggs, Kathie, p 88, 89   kjbriggs@voyager.net

Chapman, Rosie Maxine p 40, 41, 42, 43   mizrosie@sprynet.com

Chester, Amy, p 52, 53   leafshadowarts@charter.net

Cooley, Andrea, p 65-67   Fordollart@aol.com

Dahlin, Judith, p 115   DAHLIN48@msn.com

Doroshow, Dayle, p 44   dayledoroshow@hotmail.com, www.dayledorosho.com

Gerity, Lani, p 118, 119   g-l-a-g-@hotmail.com

Goodin, Cody, p 90, 91, 92   codyart@fuse.net,   www.codygoodin-fineartsphotographer.com

Hastings, Pamela, pamela@pamelahastings.com,   www.pamelahastings.com,
        http://www.pamelasjournal.blogspot.com/   http://www.hotflashwomen.blogspot.com/

Hickman, Annie, p 106   bugsandballoons@earthlink.net,   http://www.bugsandballoons.com

Hennen, Margi, p 78, 79   msmargi@mb.sympatico.ca

Kobe, Barb. p 94, 95, 96, 97   bkobe@comcast.net,   http://www.barbkobe.com

Marallo, Mariena and Partick Wadden, p 107   liveart@armofthesea.org,
        http://www.armofthesea.org

McGarvey, Eileen, p 36, 37   eileen2000@hotmail.com

McGuinness, Margaret, MA, Med, ATR-BC, pp 116, 117   m.m.mcguinness@gmail.com

Murray, Davina, p 64   mdzm@optusnet.com.au

O'Brien, Linda, p 22, 23   gourdart@burntofferings.com,   http://www.burntofferings.com

Pearce, Liz. p 125   www.heartfeltdolls.weebly.com

Pryma, Cindy, p 108, 109   cindyp@meridian.com.au

Rojas, Rosie, p 48, 49   rrojas!satx.rr.com,   http://www.asinglerose.com

Shelton, Karen, p 120, 121, 122   Littledeadgirl88@yahoo.com,
        http://littledeadgirl0.tripod.com/creepydolls/id12.html

Snow, Violet, p 104, 105   vsnow@lookseek.net

Stubblefield, Eeo, p 104, 105   eeos@ulster.net

Weinstein, Riva, p 24,25   magic_medicine_workshop@yahoo.com

Inspiring Sites and Blogs

http://learningtoloveyoumore.com/hello/index.php "the best art and writing is almost like an assignment; it is so vibrant that you feel compelled to make something in response."

http://sabrinawardharrisonart.com/ Images and writing, permission to be creative. She calls herself a Creative Pioneer and has perhaps become stunningly successful at marketing, but take a look

http://www.healingceilings.com/ Evidence-based design in health care

http://the-art-of-autism.com/ Using art with autistic people

https://www.facebook.com/groups/internationalarttherapy/permalink/10152984637471203/

http://creativeaging.org, membership@creativeaging.org

http://www.interstitialarts.org/wordpress/ Images and writing, mind-stretching stories

http://www.justanothermystery.com/ The amazing Leslie Gelber

http://www.barbkobe.com/ Lots of healing doll information

http://hotflashwomen.blogspot.com/ Pamela's blog with art/doll instruction

http://pamelasjournal.blogspot.com/ Pamela's blog with essays and family photos

https://lisafam.wordpress.com/ /art therapist and healing doll artist in Melborne

www.healingandtransformativedolls.com/ Barb Kobe's site for dolls, books, classes

www.1000journals.com/ journaling for connection and causes

www.pinterest.com/ endless online exhibits, including healing dolls

  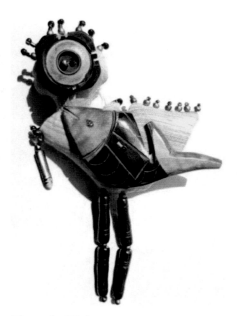

Phoenix Rising

Additional Literary Resources

Bailey, Elinor Peace. Mother Plays with Dolls. VA: EPM Publications, Inc. 1990.

Chermin, Kim. The Woman who Gave Birth to her Mother. NY: Viking, 1998.

Cassou, Michele and Chubley, Stewart. Life, Paint, and Passion. NY: Penguin Putnam, 1995.

Cosentino, Donald J., ed. Sacred Arts of Haitian Vodou. CA:UCLA Fowler Museum, 1998.

Estes, Clarissa Pinkola, Women Who Run with the Wolves. NY: Ballantine, 1992.

Flack, Audrey. Art and Soul. NY: Penguin Putnam, Inc.,1986.

Ganim, Barbara. Art and Healing. NY: Random House, Inc., 1999.

Gerity, Lani Alaine. Creativity and the Dissociative Patient. London: Jessica Kingsley Publishers, Ltd., 1999. www.slideshare.net/LaniPuppetmaker/bear_doll-Story-book?related, www.hLanipuppetmaker.blogspot.com/

Goleman, Daniel. Emotional Intelligence. NY: Bantam Books, 1997.

Hastings, Pamela. Pamela's Paper Doll Inspiration Book. NY: Pamela, 2002.

_____Pamela's Designing a Doll and Making Faces Inspiration Book. NY: Pamela 2002.

_____Hot Flash: A Celebration. WA: Pamela, 2010.

Hopke, Robert. There are No Accidents. NY: Riverhead Books, Penguin Putnam, 1997.

Kessler, Lauren. Counter Clockwise, Rodale Press, 2013.

Light, Cassandra. Way of the Doll. San Francisco: Chronicle Books, 1995.

McNiff, Shaun. Art as Medicine. CO: Shambhala, 1992.

Meyers, Tona Pearce (ed.). The Soul of creativity. CA: New World Library, 1999.

Moyers, Bill. Healing and the Mind. NY: Bantam Doubleday Dell Publishing, 1993.

Nachmanovitch, Stephen. Free Play, Improvisation in Life and Art. CA:Jeremy P. Tarcher, Inc., 1990.

Poole, William. The Heart of Healing: Institute of Noetic Sciences. Atlanta, 1993.

Prain, Leanne. Strange Material: Storytelling through Textiles. Vancouver: Arsenal Pulp Press, 2014.

Siegel, Bernie S. Love, Medicine, & Miracles. NY, CA: Harper & Row, 1986.

Tasch, Jacqueline A. (ed). Art, Rage, Us: Art and Writing by Women with Breast Cancer. Chronicle Books, San Francisco, 1998.

Wizlind, Mara. Voicing our Visions, Writings by Women Artists. NY: Universe Press, 1991.

Woronov, Mary. Wake for the Angels. MA: Journey Editions, 1994.

Zinker, Joseph. Creative Process in Gestalt Therapy. NY: Random House, 1977.

Words of Wisdom

We have the power to transform ourselves—if we want to badly enough and are willing to work at it. Changing ourselves works even though we can't change anyone else. Maybe by interacting with the world differently the chemistry with others will alter. When I found myself consistently angry with a job or a partner and felt that changing myself in those contexts would be a sell-out, I left. Being angry and feeling unable to express that is not healthy.

It can be helpful now, or at any point in the future, to revisit what you've collected in your Transformative Notebook or created. Transform a technique or pattern that you have used earlier to approach a different situation or problem. The years of studying Buddhism and practicing meditation have helped me to be more empathetic to my mother's own issues and more patient when she needs my help. As we work to put our attitudes to and relationships with others into concrete form with the work of Transformative Doll making, Empathy increasing and fear dissolving work back and forth and feed each other.

Many great discussions and insights have emerged from my classes:

"I decided to use this class as an opportunity to explore retirement/aging issues. I have been a clinical psychologist for over 20 years, and have been increasingly tired out by the demands of my profession. When I saw the doll icon project I was struck by the way the arms are tight against the body, which suggested to me a feeling of being tied up. My psychologist/healer doll wears a mask to hide her personal identity, has a string of pearls coming from the mouth, as patients expect only pearls of wisdom. She wears a golden cape, suggesting omniscient authority.

On the back, I have written in ink 'trail of fears,' referring to my anxiety/fear when I perform as this doll/role. Fears include not being perfect, and especially, suicidal patients (last year, for the first time, I suffered the tremendous loss of a patient to suicide). The red beads refer to the hot red coals of fear, which are constantly with me." Fran

This is a powerful Word Picture—an interesting group project would be to exchange verbal descriptions of a self-representative doll we are making, and have our partner do a figure from the word description, then share. People want nothing more than to be seen and heard TRUE-ly. What you give, you may receive.

Like Outsider Artists we can create for the sheer joy of the process but also to explore previously uncharted territory. We need the time and space to follow our own paths, regardless of whether or not anyone else understands. I think, I KNOW, the world needs people like us.

The in between place is important in the creative process. First confront the problem and collect material, then a period of struggle or meditation while the ideas cook, an Aha moment, lots of hard work, recovery, the cognitive processes work in the background, then perhaps more insights after the in between stage.

The Transformative Process has been a part of my life for a long time now and will never cease to be a valuable tool for me. We all have the power to transform ourselves if we want to badly enough and are willing to put in the necessary work, knowing that change is the constant in life. Changing ourselves works when we can't change anyone else—and maybe by transforming ourselves the chemistry with others will alter.

When I found myself feeling angry at my partner all the time, I took myself off to the other edge of the country. When I couldn't stand my job any more, I made it work as well as I could and saved my money until I could afford to stop. Now I am struggling with the concepts of aging and losing power—the ability to totally care for myself, move, think, and live independently.

Each stage of life, each second, involves changes and transformations—now it's aging that has my attention. Ruth Ozeki, novelist and Zen priest reminds us of her teacher, Dogan's perception of time. Each day consists of 6,400,099,980 moments, which can be frittered or savored—it's up to us.

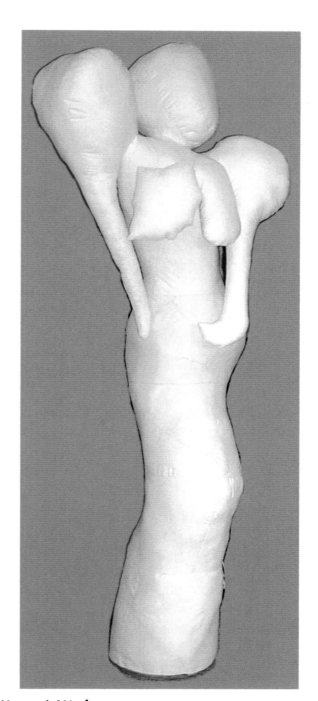

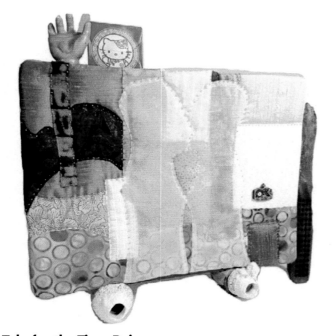

Tale for the Time Being
2015 10 Mixed media, fabric.

Women's Work
2009-2011 9.5 feet Quilt batting on a metal armature, covered with a muslin skin. My largest work, begun when I realized that the art world only paid attention to really big things and people. Now I make for my own pleasure. I named the sculpture for the thousands of tiny stitches that will never be seen or appreciated, like most of women's work. My friend, Tom Light soldered and bent the armature to scale from electrical conduit. She stood in the center of my living space, with the Thanksgiving buffet line moving around her for 3 years.

Conclusion

I have noted in my own Life Journey that the opportunities are always there, one simply must be aware and look to see them. Look at the images and joy-producing events in your life. Make change evolutionary. This Transformative Doll Making is process more than product or analysis, feeling and practicing more than learning or analysis, except for what you are teaching yourself about YOU and your expanding possibilities.

I am a facilitator and welcome you into this experience because you want to be here, not to please anyone else. Expand into your natural ability to exert power over your own past, present, and future, gain the ability to alter the ending of your story, which doesn't end until we depart this particular plane of existence.

This book is just the beginning. It is not only a road map to life change via doll making, but the winding path of my life's work, and what I might do when I grow up.

Vigil   2013   15"

I am available for teaching, facilitating group process and exhibiting.
My books, more information and art work are available at:
http://www.pamelahastings.com
http://www.hotflashwomen.blogspot.com/
http://www.pamelasjournal.blogspot.com/
pamela@pamelahastings.com
Video of me teaching gusset design: Pamela Hastings Teaching Gussets on YouTube

Liquid Planet
2015   10" mixed media   Change-the-World art?

Made in the USA
Middletown, DE
12 May 2021